WordPress Multisite Administration

A concise guide to set up, manage, and customize your blog network using WordPress multisite

Tyler L. Longren

[PACKT] open source*

PUBLISHING

community experience distilled

BIRMINGHAM - MUMBAI

WordPress Multisite Administration

First published: August 2013

Production Reference: 1190813

Published by Packt Publishing Ltd.
Livery Place
35 Livery Street
Birmingham B3 2PB, UK.

ISBN 978-1-78328-247-0

www.packtpub.com

Cover Image by Karl Moore (karl.moore@ukonline.co.uk)

Credits

Author
Tyler L. Longren

Reviewers
David Kryzaniak

Mario Peshev

Acquisition Editors
Martin Bell

Julian Ursell

Commissioning Editor
Sharvari Tawde

Technical Editors
Krutika Parab

Hardik B. Soni

Dennis John

Project Coordinator
Amigya Khurana

Proofreader
Stephen Copestake

Indexer
Hemangini Bari

Production Coordinator
Adonia Jones

Cover Work
Adonia Jones

About the Author

Tyler L. Longren grew up in Central Iowa and continues to reside and make a living there. He's worked for various employers, from newspapers and commercial kitchens to startups and well-established Internet companies.

Tyler has been involved in technology since he was very young and remembers watching his father write software from as early as 2 years old. Tyler was fortunate to attend a primary school where he was able to explore his interests more freely than might have been possible elsewhere.

Since 1999, Tyler has been especially interested in web development. He's worked on all types of websites, websites for friends, local companies, and high-traffic niche websites. He's been using WordPress since 2005, back when WordPress required PHP4 and would not work with PHP5. He's also been an avid blogger since 2002 and started with some custom PHP and an old HP Vectra XW machine running Slackware Linux out of his home, with a dedicated phone line for the modem.

I would like to thank my family for their support, especially my wife Kayla and our daughter, Sydney, who insists on staying out catching lightning bugs until 10 p.m. every night.

About the Reviewers

David Kryzaniak is a programming ninja at Blue Door Consulting in Oshkosh, Wisconsin. He holds a BS in Information Science from UW Green Bay; while he's primarily a PHP developer, he tends to do a lot of frontend (CSS, jQuery, responsive web design) work too. He enjoys playing with electronics, hacking into things he shouldn't, and doing a little (ok… a lot of) WordPress development. His super-awesome-way-cool-can't-miss-it blog is `http://dave.kz`.

Mario Peshev is a WordPress engineer and open source consultant. He is the lead tech guy at DevriX, a small consulting agency focusing on WordPress development and architecture, consulting and migrating businesses to open source platforms.

Mario has been working in the IT field for the past 13 years. He is certified in Java programming and Secure Web engineering and experienced in Java, PHP, Python, and JavaScript development. He is also a part-time trainer with 7 years of training experience and has taught dozens of technical classes in technical schools and universities and organizations and companies such as Saudi Aramco, The European Organization for Nuclear Research (CERN), VMware, Software AG, and Melexis Microelectronic Systems. His passion for open source is contagious.

www.PacktPub.com

Support files, eBooks, discount offers and more

You might want to visit www.PacktPub.com for support files and downloads related to your book.

Did you know that Packt offers eBook versions of every book published, with PDF and ePub files available? You can upgrade to the eBook version at www.PacktPub.com and as a print book customer, you are entitled to a discount on the eBook copy. Get in touch with us at service@packtpub.com for more details.

At www.PacktPub.com, you can also read a collection of free technical articles, sign up for a range of free newsletters and receive exclusive discounts and offers on Packt books and eBooks.

http://PacktLib.PacktPub.com

Do you need instant solutions to your IT questions? PacktLib is Packt's online digital book library. Here, you can access, read and search across Packt's entire library of books.

Why Subscribe?

- Fully searchable across every book published by Packt
- Copy and paste, print and bookmark content
- On-demand and accessible via web browser

Free Access for Packt account holders

If you have an account with Packt at www.PacktPub.com, you can use this to access PacktLib today and view nine entirely free books. Simply use your login credentials for immediate access.

Table of Contents

Preface

Surely you're familiar with `WordPress.com`, the ultra popular blogging network. Most people don't realize that the software behind WordPress is available for anyone to use, allowing anyone to create a blog network similar to `WordPress.com`.

WordPress multisite is at the core of `WordPress.com` and comes as part of the standard self-hosted WordPress download from `WordPress.org`. We can use WordPress multisite for a number of purposes, from setting up a public blog network by consolidating all of your single site WordPress installations into a multisite network.

WordPress multisite administration will take you through everything you need to know about WordPress multisite. You'll need to have a little experience with single site WordPress installations, but that's it. We cover topics like activating multisite from a single site installation, setting up a custom author-listing directory, and protecting your multisite network.

What this book covers

Chapter 1, Getting Started with WordPress Multisite, will cover activating WordPress multisite from a single-site installation, and other basic tasks.

Chapter 2, Customization, will guide you in installing and configuring themes and plugins. We'll also go over how to create a custom author-listing directory.

Chapter 3, User Management and Permissions, will help you understand what the Super Administrator is and everything it can do. We'll also touch on individual site management and go over other user roles and permissions.

Chapter 4, Protecting Your Multisite Network, will focus on the best practices for keeping your multisite installation secure; from plugins to password protection with the .htaccess files.

Chapter 5, Migrating Multiple WordPress Blogs to a Multisite Network, will cover everything you need to bring multiple, single-site WordPress blogs over to a multisite network. Makes updating everything at once really easy.

Chapter 6, Site Optimization, will cover various ways you can enhance the performance of your sites. Everything from using CDN services like CloudFlare to caching plugins for WordPress.

Chapter 7, Troubleshooting and Maintaining Stability, will focus on common problems and fixes for those problems. We'll also go over backups and updating WordPress.

What you need for this book

You'll need to have a place to host your website, first of all. If you don't have a webhost, you can follow along by installing a web server, PHP, and MySQL on your computer. This can be achieved through a variety of methods, including Google LAMP, and you'll find many options.

You'll also need some sort of FTP client; I use FileZilla throughout the book. A text editor or other code editor will also be needed; I used Sublime Text in the book.

Who this book is for

This book is geared towards people who have some experience with WordPress already. You don't need to know anything about WordPress multisite, though.

People who run multiple WordPress single-site installations will be especially interested, since we cover how to migrate those single sites over to a multisite network. Merging all your sites into one network makes updating and general maintenance really, really easy.

Conventions

In this book, you will find a number of styles of text that distinguish between different kinds of information. Here are some examples of these styles, and an explanation of their meaning.

Code words in text, database table names, folder names, filenames, file extensions, pathnames, dummy URLs, user input, and Twitter handles are shown as follows: "There's a comment in there that says `Multisite` and directly under it is where we define the named constant, `WP_ALLOW_MULTISITE`, to `true`."

A block of code is set as follows:

```
// ** MySQL settings - You can get this info from your web host ** //
/** The name of the database for WordPress */
define('DB_NAME', 'database_name_here');

/** MySQL database username */
define('DB_USER', 'username_here');

/** MySQL database password */
define('DB_PASSWORD', 'password_here');

/** MySQL hostname */
define('DB_HOST', 'localhost');

/** Database Charset to use in creating database tables. */
define('DB_CHARSET', 'utf8');

/** The Database Collate type. Don't change this if in doubt. */
define('DB_COLLATE', '');

/* Multisite */
define('WP_ALLOW_MULTISITE', true);
```

New terms and **important words** are shown in bold. Words that you see on the screen, in menus or dialog boxes for example, appear in the text like this: "Specify your **Network Title** and **Admin E-mail Address** values, and click on the **Install** button at the bottom of the form."

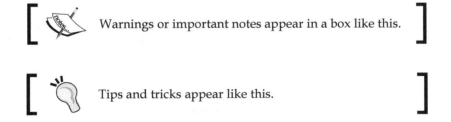

> Warnings or important notes appear in a box like this.

> Tips and tricks appear like this.

Reader feedback

Feedback from our readers is always welcome. Let us know what you think about this book—what you liked or may have disliked. Reader feedback is important for us to develop titles that you really get the most out of.

To send us general feedback, simply send an e-mail to feedback@packtpub.com, and mention the book title via the subject of your message.

If there is a topic that you have expertise in and you are interested in either writing or contributing to a book, see our author guide on www.packtpub.com/authors.

Customer support

Now that you are the proud owner of a Packt book, we have a number of things to help you to get the most from your purchase.

Downloading the example code

You can download the example code files for all Packt books you have purchased from your account at http://www.packtpub.com. If you purchased this book elsewhere, you can visit http://www.packtpub.com/support and register to have the files e-mailed directly to you.

Errata

Although we have taken every care to ensure the accuracy of our content, mistakes do happen. If you find a mistake in one of our books—maybe a mistake in the text or the code—we would be grateful if you would report this to us. By doing so, you can save other readers from frustration and help us improve subsequent versions of this book. If you find any errata, please report them by visiting http://www.packtpub.com/submit-errata, selecting your book, clicking on the **errata submission form** link, and entering the details of your errata. Once your errata are verified, your submission will be accepted and the errata will be uploaded on our website, or added to any list of existing errata, under the Errata section of that title. Any existing errata can be viewed by selecting your title from http://www.packtpub.com/support.

Piracy

Piracy of copyright material on the Internet is an ongoing problem across all media. At Packt, we take the protection of our copyright and licenses very seriously. If you come across any illegal copies of our works, in any form, on the Internet, please provide us with the location address or website name immediately so that we can pursue a remedy.

Please contact us at copyright@packtpub.com with a link to the suspected pirated material.

We appreciate your help in protecting our authors, and our ability to bring you valuable content.

Questions

You can contact us at questions@packtpub.com if you are having a problem with any aspect of the book, and we will do our best to address it.

1
Getting Started with WordPress Multisite

WordPress is an amazing piece of software. One of its more advanced features is called **multisite**. With WordPress multisite, you can essentially build your own blog network, similar to Wordpress.com or Tumblr.

System requirements and considerations

Multisite is an integrated part of the WordPress core. That means you won't have to download anything other than the official WordPress package to get set up. There are some basic system requirements that you should consider before even trying to install WordPress. At the most basic level, WordPress requires PHP 5.2.4 or greater and MySQL 5.0 or greater. You can see a detailed list of system requirements at http://wordpress.org/about/requirements/.

There are some basic things you should take into consideration before deciding to use WordPress multisite for your project. Most important is defining a project scope and making sure that WordPress provides enough features to meet that scope. It's possible that WordPress is overkill, in terms of features, for your project as well. It's all really dictated by the specific features your project needs.

Chances are, since you're reading this book, you want to set up a blog network of some type. WordPress multisite is used for a wide variety of reasons, from university class blogs to high-traffic websites or anything in between. The most common use of WordPress multisite I've seen is with small groups of individuals who want a blog but don't want to join a massive blog network such as WordPress.com.

WordPress didn't always include the multisite feature. Prior to WordPress 3.0, WordPress came in two flavors, **regular** and **multiuser**. WordPress 3.0 introduced WordPress multisite, as it's known today. WordPress 3.0 was released in June 17, 2010.

Terminology

There are going to be some basic WordPress-related terms that you'll want to become familiar with. These terms usually apply to multisite and a standard WordPress single-site install. You can check some of the terminologies used in WordPress at `http://codex.wordpress.org/WordPress_Semantics`.

Now that you've got some basic WordPress knowledge, we might as well get to downloading and installing WordPress. The WordPress installation process is very easy, only requiring you to upload the files to your webhost and then to edit database connection settings in a file named `wp-config.php`.

Before we get too far, we need to take a couple things into consideration. First, think about how you want URLs to be set up. You can use subdomains for each individual's blog URL or you can use a subfolder style setup, such as `http://multisite.longren.org/tyler/`. Also, installing themes and plugins is a bit different from a typical WordPress install, but we'll get to that a bit later in this chapter. I really suggest reading the *Before You Create A Network* article in the WordPress Codex, available at `http://codex.wordpress.org/Before_You_Create_A_Network`.

Okay, let's get down to installing WordPress and enabling the multisite feature.

Installing WordPress

We'll start the WordPress installation wizard with the web browser. I like to use Google Chrome but any web browser should work. So, open your browser and navigate to your multisite installation URL. I installed WordPress multisite at a subdomain of my main `longren.org` domain name, but you can use a subdirectory too, such as `http://www.longren.org/multisite/`.

Once you've opened your site you'll see a window as shown in the following screenshot. This is where you can set the name of the site as well as choose your administrative username and password. The default administrative username in WordPress is `admin` but I highly suggest that you change that to something else. A lot of WordPress web attacks try to exploit the default administrative account name, so not having an `admin` user puts you in a better position security-wise.

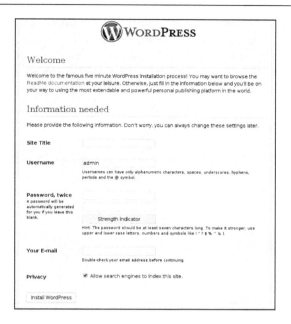

That is the only page where you need to enter any information in the WordPress installation wizard. In the next screenshot, you can see what the page in the previous screenshot should look like after you've filled everything out.

After you've filled everything out and chosen a username anything *other than* the
admin term, click on the **Install WordPress** button at the bottom of that page. After
clicking on **Install WordPress**, you'll see a **Success**! message along with your chosen
username. As you can see in the following screenshot, your password isn't shown on
the screen:

Once you're on the **Success!** page, you can click on the **Log In** button. You'll be taken
to your WordPress login page, located at /wp-login.php or http://multisite.
longren.org/wp-login.php in my example. You can also navigate to /wp-admin/
or http://multisite.longren.org/wp-admin/, to log in to your WordPress
Dashboard window. The default login page can be seen in the following screenshot.
The login screen can be changed visually through the use of plugins or custom
settings for your WordPress theme.

Enter the **Username** and **Password** values that you chose when going through the WordPress installation wizard to get logged in. Upon successful login, you'll be taken to your WordPress **Dashboard** window for the first time. Now, we get to do more stuff that's specific to multisite setups. But first, the following screenshot shows what your WordPress **Dashboard** window should look like:

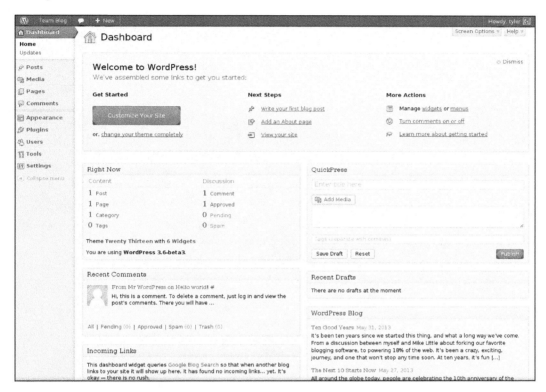

Configuring the WordPress multisite feature

First, we need to download WordPress. Open your web browser and navigate to `http://wordpress.org/download/`. At that page you can choose to download WordPress as a ZIP file or as a `.tar.gz` file. If you're on Windows you'll probably want to download the ZIP file, while Linux and OS X users can download whichever they prefer.

Once you've got the .zip or .tar.gz file downloaded, open it up and you should see a folder named wordpress in there. Extract that wordpress folder to somewhere on your local computer, such as your desktop. Next, open up an FTP connection to your webhost and upload everything from the wordpress directory that we have put on your desktop earlier.

After the upload is finished, go ahead and install WordPress as you would for a single site. After that install is done, we'll edit wp-config.php to enable multisite.

We'll go through the basic settings in wp-config.php, including code snippets.

After renaming wp-config-sample.php to wp-config.php, open it up for editing. You can open it directly from your webhost if you're using a FTP client such as FileZilla. Just right-click on wp-config.php and select **View/Edit** within FileZilla. I chose to use FileZilla as an example because it's available for multiple operating systems, including Windows, OS X, and Linux.

Once you've opened wp-config.php in your text editor, you'll be presented with some code that looks like what you'll see in the next code.

```
// ** MySQL settings - You can get this info from your web host ** //
/** The name of the database for WordPress */
define('DB_NAME', 'database_name_here');

/** MySQL database username */
define('DB_USER', 'username_here');

/** MySQL database password */
define('DB_PASSWORD', 'password_here');

/** MySQL hostname */
define('DB_HOST', 'localhost');

/** Database Charset to use in creating database tables. */
define('DB_CHARSET', 'utf8');

/** The Database Collate type. Don't change this if in doubt. */
define('DB_COLLATE', '');

/* Multisite */
define('WP_ALLOW_MULTISITE', true);

/**#@+
```

```
 * Authentication Unique Keys and Salts.
 *
 * Change these to different unique phrases!
 * You can generate these using the {@link https://api.wordpress.org/
secret-key/1.1/salt/ WordPress.org secret-key service}
 * You can change these at any point in time to invalidate all
existing cookies. This will force all users to have to log in again.
 *
 * @since 2.6.0
 */
define('AUTH_KEY',          'put your unique phrase here');
define('SECURE_AUTH_KEY',   'put your unique phrase here');
define('LOGGED_IN_KEY',     'put your unique phrase here');
define('NONCE_KEY',         'put your unique phrase here');
define('AUTH_SALT',         'put your unique phrase here');
define('SECURE_AUTH_SALT',  'put your unique phrase here');
define('LOGGED_IN_SALT',    'put your unique phrase here');
define('NONCE_SALT',        'put your unique phrase here');
```

You may notice that there's an additional piece of code in there, compared to what's being shown in your wp-config.php file. There's a comment in there that says Multisite and directly under it is where we define the named constant, WP_ALLOW_MULTISITE, to true. In the following code, you'll find exactly what you need to add to wp-config.php to enable the multisite feature:

```
/* Multisite */
define('WP_ALLOW_MULTISITE', true);
```

I like to set that constant below the database config settings, around lines 36 and 37 in the default wp-config.php file.

The database configuration constants at the top of wp-config.php are pretty self-explanatory. They're named things such as DB_NAME, DB_USER, and DB_PASSWORD. Bet you can guess what those values should be set to. There are some not quite so obvious database settings too, such as DB_CHARSET and DB_COLLATE. It's usually a good idea to keep those at the default value; DB_CHARSET is set to utf8 by default, which is Unicode. The DB_COLLATE constant should contain a value for the language you're going to use within WordPress. If you're using English, you can just leave the value for DB_COLLATE blank.

In the following code, I also included a bunch of named constants for **authentication unique keys and salts,** towards the bottom. You need to change the existing values there. You can easily generate new, random values by visiting `https://api.wordpress.org/secret-key/1.1/salt/`. Just copy the eight lines of code generated on that page and then paste it into `wp-config.php`, replacing the other keys. So you should go from the following code to something resembling what you see in the version generated by `api.wordpress.com`:

```
define('AUTH_KEY',         'put your unique phrase here');
define('SECURE_AUTH_KEY',  'put your unique phrase here');
define('LOGGED_IN_KEY',    'put your unique phrase here');
define('NONCE_KEY',        'put your unique phrase here');
define('AUTH_SALT',        'put your unique phrase here');
define('SECURE_AUTH_SALT', 'put your unique phrase here');
define('LOGGED_IN_SALT',   'put your unique phrase here');
define('NONCE_SALT',       'put your unique phrase here');
```

And following is the code that's an example of the keys generated on the `api.wordpress.com` page:

```
define('AUTH_KEY',         '*`b7,!cuc2Ub+IabKJ-h|*5SdfO8uBm-
L1&=<Q5>6oiS3?qCTVA|^d%W(o[<Y-<C');
define('SECURE_AUTH_KEY',  '<v?OP<V*:Nz#AazY0l?*7^{d-i6-
EyA*,|Flp>|BR&*u=&Gad{2r6L^8g+#r~Z&^');
define('LOGGED_IN_KEY',    'I!u|T-h(4kc[ L%#QJs7`NyM.]]-W`/,rmhRteNQ`^
LC+0>0&zG|6Lqe5Zf%kx$B');
define('NONCE_KEY',        ',[RGlO?&-GDw|>DC&rH5gMQ040(d3Xo{dCAY~F2
8M=:=]l>/_,|d#19X_aRTHfnp');
define('AUTH_SALT',        '8G+g,K.Sd^PDyD,q@,mcXs&CxqR5veL*z9P%<O|+O2
^YU}Ob^je|Ty;{JL1AQOz/');
define('SECURE_AUTH_SALT', 'mndP#V.PZNH+N2HN9,I5`KC_;|j7TyT[`_1UFX
3j|x18*cZSO5`u2j5miB^~d^:');
define('LOGGED_IN_SALT',   '[>uO+hz%+0t9X1tf<P*Sx1q44leN_WI4$l>yD-
fiu7a>{Gq+ubtqjpym4[S0YPTp');
define('NONCE_SALT',       'O -Gk@XjD{4PAi-*Q+OhVD^+6@C]Uebrwc}
qLW,2tR*1g4+NMF(sbrp>ppoFD[j');
```

After making those changes to `wp-config.php`, save the file and upload it back to your server. If you opened `wp-config.php` directly with FileZilla, you'll be prompted with a window inside FileZilla that's titled **File has changed**. This window asks if you want to upload the changed file back to the server. Click on **Yes** and your modified `wp-config.php` file will be automatically uploaded to its original location on your server. Any additional changes you make to `wp-config.php` can be uploaded simply by saving `wp-config.php` again and telling FileZilla to upload your changed file.

Now that our `wp-config.php` file knows that we're going to set up multisite, it's time to run the network setup. To install a network, start out by putting your mouse cursor over the **Tools** menu on the left-hand side of the WordPress **Dashboard** window and clicking on the **Network Setup** submenu item.

The page you're taken to after clicking on the **Network Setup** submenu item is titled **Create a Network of WordPress Sites**. Sounds awesome, right? This is ultimately what we're here for, after all.

From here, you can specify if you want to use a subdomain for individual sites or if you'd rather use a directory. I've chosen to use a directory as I think that's the most common setup. So, the URLs in my example will be `http://multisite.longren.org/tyler/` for my blog, `http://multisite.longren.org/kayla/` for my wife, Kayla's, and `http://multisite.longren.org/sydney/` for my daughter, Sydney's.

The setup I'm using on the **Create a Network of WordPress Sites** page can be seen in the following screenshot:

Specify your **Network Title** and **Admin E-mail Address** values and click on the **Install** button at the bottom of the form. After clicking on **Install** you'll see a page with **Enabling the Network** in bold at the top, with some more named constants being defined also. Copy and paste the code from the section **1** into your `wp-config.php` file and re-upload it to your server. Next, edit your `.htaccess` file. It should be in the same folder as `wp-config.php`. If the `.htaccess` file doesn't exist, you can save a blank text file as `.htaccess` and upload it to your server. Copy the Apache rewrite rules from the section **2** into your `.htaccess` file and upload it to your server, again, in the same directory as the `wp-config.php` file.

The following screenshot shows the page after clicking on **Install**; it's the page that provides the sections **1** and **2**, that I previously referenced:

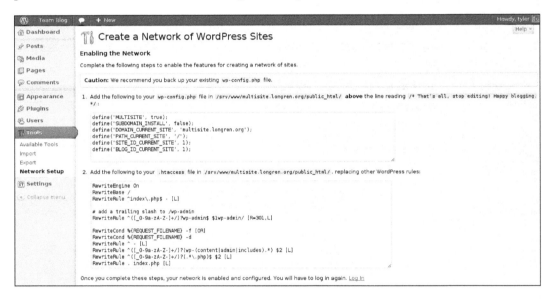

After you've uploaded your modified `wp-config.php` and `.htaccess` files, the setup of your multisite network is complete. You'll need to log in again, so just click on the **Log In** link at the very end of the **Enabling the Network** page. You'll be taken to the login page as shown previously. You may need to clear the cache in your browser and possibly delete cookies for the domain your WordPress site is using.

After you're logged back in, you should see a **My Sites** link in the WordPress toolbar at the top-left corner of the screen. Put your mouse cursor over it and then click on the **Network Admin** item. Doing so will take you to the network **Dashboard** window, which is similar in appearance to the regular WordPress **Dashboard** window but significantly different in content. This is where you can see the sites hosted by your new network. From here, you can add new sites, new users, or enable and disable themes and plugins. Cool, huh? The following is the screenshot of the network **Dashboard** window:

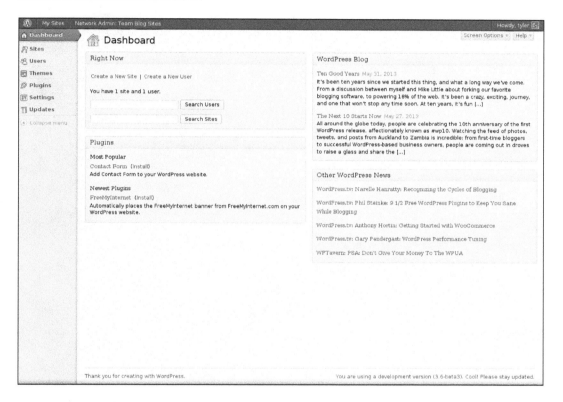

Downloading the example code

You can download the example code files for all Packt books you have purchased from your account at http://www.packtpub. com. If you purchased this book elsewhere, you can visit http://www.packtpub.com/support and register to have the files e-mailed directly to you.

Summary

Congratulations! You've created your first WordPress multisite network! Wasn't too bad, was it? In the next chapter, you'll use the knowledge gained here to really put multisite to use. We'll be covering customization, including building out a custom **Blog Directory** page, with Gravatar support and all.

2
Customization

Now that you've got a working multisite installation, we can start to add some customizations. Customizations can come in a few different forms. You're probably aware of the customizations that can be made via WordPress plugins and custom WordPress themes. Another way we can customize a multisite installation is by creating a landing page that displays information about each blog in the multisite network, as well as displaying information about the author for that individual blog.

I wrote a blog post shortly after WordPress 3.0 came out detailing how to set this landing page up. At the time, I was working for a local newspaper and we were setting up a blog network for some of our reporters to blog about politics (being in Iowa, politics are a pretty big deal here, especially around Caucus time). You can find the post at `http://www.longren.org/how-to-wordpress-3-0-multi-site-blog-directory/` if you'd like to read it. There's also a `blog-directory.zip` file attached to the post that you can download and use as a starting point.

Before we get into creating the landing page, let's get the really simple stuff out of the way and briefly go over how themes and plugins are managed in WordPress multisite installations. We'll start with themes. Themes can be activated network-wide, which is really nice if you have a theme that you want every site in your blog network to use. You can also activate a theme for an individual blog, instead of activating the theme for the entire network. This is helpful if one or two individual blogs need to have a totally unique theme that you don't want to be available to the other blogs.

Theme management

You can install themes on a multisite installation the same way you would with a regular WordPress install. Just upload the theme folder to your `wp-content/themes` folder to install the theme. Installing a theme is only part of the process for individual blogs to use the themes; you'll need to activate them for the entire blog network or for specific blogs.

To activate a theme for an entire network, click on **Themes** and then click on **Installed Themes** in the **Network Admin** dashboard. Check the themes that you want to enable, select **Network Enable** in the **Bulk Actions** drop-down menu, and then click on the **Apply** button. That's all there is to activating a theme (or multiple themes) for an entire multisite network. The individual blog owners can apply the theme just as you would in a regular, nonmultisite WordPress installation.

To activate a theme for just one specific blog and not the entire network, locate the target blog using the **Sites** menu option in the **Network Admin** dashboard. After you've found it, put your mouse cursor over the blog URL or domain. You should see the action menu appear immediately under the blog URL or domain. The action menu includes options such as **Edit**, **Dashboard**, and **Deactivate**. Click on the **Edit** action menu item and then navigate to the **Themes** tab. To activate an individual theme, just click on **Enable** below the theme that you want to activate. Or, if you want to activate multiple themes for the blog, check all the themes you want through the checkboxes on the left-hand side of each theme from the list, select **Enable** in the **Bulk Actions** drop-down menu, and then click on the **Apply** button. An important thing to keep in mind is that themes that have been activated for the entire network won't be shown here. Now the blog administrator can apply the theme to their blog just as they normally would.

Plugin management

To install a plugin for network use, upload the plugin folder to `wp-content/plugins/` as you normally would. Unlike themes, plugins cannot be activated on a per-site basis. As network administrator, you can add a plugin to the **Plugins** page for all sites, but you can't make a plugin available to one specific site. It's all or nothing.

You'll also want to make sure that you've enabled the **Plugins** page for the sites that need it. You can enable the **Plugins** page by visiting the **Network Admin** dashboard and then navigating to the **Network Settings** page. At the bottom of that page you should see a **Menu Settings** section where you can check a box next to **Plugins** to enable the plugins page. Make sure to click on the **Save Changes** button at the bottom or nothing will change. You can see the **Menu Settings** section in the following screenshot. That's where you'll want to enable the **Plugins** page.

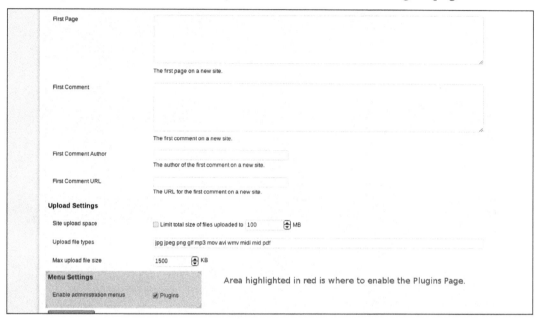

Enabling the Plugins page

After you've ensured that the **Plugins** page is enabled, specific site administrators will be able to enable or disable plugins as they normally would.

To enable a plugin for the entire network go to the **Network Admin** dashboard, mouse over the **Plugins** menu item, and then click on **Installed Plugins**. This will look pretty familiar to you; it looks pretty much like the **Installed Plugins** page does on a typical WordPress single-site installation. The following screenshot shows the installed **Plugins** page:

Enable plugins for the entire network

You'll notice below each plugin there's some text that reads **Network Activate**. I bet you can guess what clicking that will do. Yes, clicking on the **Network Activate** link will activate that plugin for the entire network.

That's all there is to the basic plugin setup in WordPress multisite. There's another plugin feature that is often overlooked in WordPress multisite, and that's must-use plugins. These are plugins that are required for every blog or site on the network.

Must-use plugins can be installed in the `wp-content/mu-plugins/` folder but they must be single-file plugins. The files within folders won't be read. You can't deactivate or activate the must-use plugins. If they exist in the `mu-plugins` folder, they're used. They're entirely hidden from the **Plugin** pages, so individual site administrators won't even see them or know they're there. I don't think must-use plugins are a commonly used thing, but it's nice information to have just in case. Some plugins, especially domain mapping plugins, need to be installed in `mu-plugins` and need to be activated before the normal plugins.

Third-party plugins and plugins for plugin management

We should also discuss some of the plugins that are available for making the management of plugins and themes on WordPress multisite installations a bit easier. One of the most popular plugins is called **Multisite Plugin Manager**, and is developed by *Aaron Edwards* of UglyRobot.com. The Multisite Plugin Manager plugin was previously known as WPMU Plugin Manager. The plugin can be obtained from the WordPress Plugin Directory at http://wordpress.org/plugins/multisite-plugin-manager/. Here's a quick rundown of some of the plugin features:

- Select which plugins specific sites have access to
- Set certain plugins to autoactivate itself for new blogs or sites
- Activate/deactivate a plugin on all network sites
- Assign some special plugin access permissions to specific network sites

Another plugin that you may find useful is called **WordPress MU Domain Mapping**. It allows you to easily map any blog or site to an external domain. You can find this plugin in the WordPress Plugin Directory at http://wordpress.org/plugins/wordpress-mu-domain-mapping/.

There's one other plugin I want to mention; the only drawback is that it's not a free plugin. It's called **WP Multisite Replicator**, and you can probably guess what it does. This plugin will allow you to set up a "template" blog or site and then replicate that site when adding new sites or blogs. The idea is that you'd create a blog or site that has all the features that other sites in your network will need. Then, you can easily replicate that site when creating a new site or blog. It will copy widgets, themes, and plugin settings to the new site or blog, which makes deploying new, identical sites extremely easy. It's not an expensive plugin, costing about $36 at the moment of writing, which is well worth it in my opinion if you're going to be creating lots of sites that have the same basic feature set. WP Multisite Replicator can be found at http://wpebooks.com/replicator/.

Creating a blog directory / landing page

Now that we've got the basic theme and plugin stuff taken care of, I think it's time to move onto creating a blog directory or a landing page, whichever you prefer to call it. From this point on I'll be referring to it as a blog directory. You can see a basic version of what we're going to make in the following screenshot. The users on my example multisite installation, at `http://multisite.longren.org/`, are Kayla and Sydney, my wife and daughter.

Blog directory example

As I mentioned earlier in this chapter, I wrote a post about creating this blog directory back when WordPress 3.0 was first released in 2010. I'll be using that post as the basis for most of what we'll do to create the blog directory with some things changed around, so this will integrate more nicely into whatever theme you're using on the main network site.

The first thing we need to do is to create a basic WordPress page template that we can apply to a newly created WordPress page. This template will contain the HTML structure for the blog directory and will dictate where the blog names will be shown and where the recent posts and blog description will be displayed.

There's no reason that you need to stick with the following blog directory template specifically. You can take the code and add or remove various elements, such as the recent post if you don't want to show them.

You'll want to implement this blog directory template as a child theme in WordPress. To do that, just make a new folder in `wp-content/themes/`. I typically name my child theme folders after their parent themes. So, the child theme folder I made was `wp-content/themes/twentythirteen-tyler/`.

Once you've got the child theme folder created, make a new file called `style.css` and make sure it has the following code at the top:

```
/*
Theme Name:      Twenty Thirteen Child Theme
Theme URI:       http://yourdomain.com
Description:     Child theme for the Twenty Thirteen theme
Author:          Your name here
Author URI:      http://example.com/about/
Template:        twentythirteen
Version:         0.1.0
*/

/* ================ */
/* = The 1Kb Grid = */     /* 12 columns, 60 pixels each, with 20
pixel gutter */
/* ================ */

.grid_1 { width:60px; }
.grid_2 { width:140px; }
.grid_3 { width:220px; }
.grid_4 { width:300px; }
.grid_5 { width:380px; }
.grid_6 { width:460px; }
.grid_7 { width:540px; }
.grid_8 { width:620px; }
.grid_9 { width:700px; }
.grid_10 { width:780px; }
.grid_11 { width:860px; }
.grid_12 { width:940px; }

.column {
margin: 0 10px;
overflow: hidden;
float: left;
display: inline;
}
.row {
width: 960px;
margin: 0 auto;
overflow: hidden;
}
```

```
.row .row {
margin: 0 -10px;
width: auto;
display: inline-block;
}
.author_bio {
border: 1px solid #e7e7e7;
margin-top: 10px;
padding-top: 10px;
background:#ffffff url('images/sign.png') no-repeat right bottom;
z-index: -99999;
}
small { font-size: 12px; }
.post_count {
text-align: center;
font-size: 10px;
font-weight: bold;
line-height: 15px;
text-transform: uppercase;
float: right;
margin-top: -65px;
margin-right: 20px;
}
.post_count a {
color: #000;
}
#content a {
text-decoration: none;
-webkit-transition: text-shadow .1s linear;
outline: none;
}

#content a:hover {
color: #2DADDA;
text-shadow: 0 0 6px #278EB3;
}
```

The preceding code adds the styling to your child theme, and also tells WordPress the name of your child theme. You can set a custom theme name if you want by changing the Theme Name line to whatever you like. The only fields in that big comment block that are required are the Theme Name and Template. Template, which should be set to whatever the parent theme's folder name is.

Now create another file in your child theme folder and name it `blog-directory.php`. The remaining blocks of code need to go into that `blog-directory.php` file:

```php
<?php
/**
 * Template Name: Blog Directory
 *
 * A custom page template with a sidebar.
 * Selectable from a dropdown menu on the add/edit page screen.
 *
 * @package WordPress
 * @subpackage Twenty Thirteen
 */
?>
<?php get_header(); ?>
<div id="container" class="onecolumn">
<div id="content" role="main">
<?php the_post(); ?>
<div id="post-<?php the_ID(); ?>" <?php post_class(); ?>>
<?php if ( is_front_page() ) { ?>
<h2 class="entry-title"><?php the_title(); ?></h2>
<?php } else { ?>
<h1 class="entry-title"><?php the_title(); ?></h1>
<?php } ?>
<div class="entry-content">
<!-- start blog directory -->
<?php
// Get the authors from the database ordered randomly
global $wpdb;
$query = "SELECT ID, user_nicename from $wpdb->users WHERE ID != '1'
ORDER BY RAND() LIMIT 50";
$author_ids = $wpdb->get_results($query);

// Loop through each author
foreach($author_ids as $author) {
// Get user data
$curauth = get_userdata($author->ID);

// Get link to author page
$user_link = get_author_posts_url($curauth->ID);
```

```
// Get blog details for the authors primary blog ID
$blog_details = get_blog_details($curauth->primary_blog);

$postText = "posts";
if ($blog_details->post_count == "1") {
  $postText = "post";
}
$updatedOn = strftime("%m/%d/%Y at %1:%M %p",strtotime($blog_details-
>last_updated));
if ($blog_details->post_count == "") {
$blog_details->post_count = "0";
}
$posts = $wpdb->get_col( "SELECT ID FROM wp_".$curauth->primary_
blog."_posts WHERE post_status='publish' AND post_type='post' AND
post_author='$author->ID' ORDER BY ID DESC LIMIT 5");
$postHTML = "";
$i=0;
foreach($posts as $p) {
$postdetail=get_blog_post($curauth->primary_blog,$p);
if ($i==0) {
$updatedOn = strftime("%m/%d/%Y at %1:%M %p",strtotime($postdetail-
>post_date));
}
$postHTML .= "&#149; <a href=\"$postdetail->guid\">$postdetail->post_
title</a><br />";
$i++;
}
?>
```

The preceding code sets up the theme and queries the WordPress database for authors. In WordPress multisite, users who have the Author permission type have a blog on the network. There's also code for grabbing posts from each of the network sites for displaying the recent posts from them:

```
<div class="author_bio">
<div class="row">
<div class="column grid_2">
<a href="<?php echo $blog_details->siteurl; ?>"><?php echo get_
avatar($curauth->user_email, '96','http://www.gravatar.com/avatar/
ad516503a11cd5ca435acc9bb6523536'); ?></a>
</div>
<div class="column grid_6">
<a href="<?php echo $blog_details->siteurl; ?>" title="<?php echo
$curauth->display_name; ?> - <?=$blog_details->blogname?>"><?php //
echo $curauth->display_name; ?> <?=$curauth->display_name;?></a><br />
```

```
<small><strong>Updated <?=$updatedOn?></strong></small><br />
<?php echo $curauth->description; ?>
</div>
<div class="column grid_3">
<h3>Recent Posts</h3>
<?=$postHTML?>
</div>
</div>
<span class="post_count"><a href="<?php echo $blog_details->siteurl;
?>" title="<?php echo $curauth->display_name; ?>"><?=$blog_details-
>post_count?><br /><?=$postText?></a></span>
</div>
<?php } ?>
<!-- end blog directory -->
<?php wp_link_pages( array( 'before' => '<div class="page-link">' .
__( 'Pages:', 'twentythirteen' ), 'after' => '</div>' ) ); ?>
<?php edit_post_link( __( 'Edit', 'twentythirteen' ), '<span
class="edit-link">', '</span>' ); ?>
</div><!-- .entry-content -->
</div><!-- #post-<?php the_ID(); ?> -->
<?php comments_template( '', true ); ?>
</div><!-- #content -->
</div><!-- #container -->
<?php //get_sidebar(); ?>
<?php get_footer(); ?>
```

Once you've got your blog-directory.php template file created, we can get actually started by setting up the page to serve as our blog directory. You'll need to set the root site's theme to your child theme; do it just as you would on a nonmultisite WordPress installation.

Before we go further, let's create a couple of network sites so we have something to see on our blog directory.

Go to the **Network Admin** dashboard, mouse over the **Sites** menu option in the left-hand side menu, and then click on **Add New**. If you're using a directory network type, as I am, the value you enter for the **Site Address** field will be the path to the directory that site sits in. So, if you enter `tyler` as the **Site Address** value, that the site can be reached at `http://multisite.longren.org/tyler/`. The settings that I used to set up `multisite.longren.org/tyler/` can be seen in the following screenshot. You'll probably want to add a couple of sites just so you get a good idea of what your blog directory page will look like.

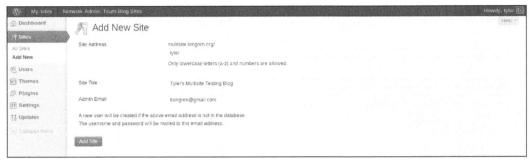

Example individual site setup

Now we can set up the actual blog directory page. On the main dashboard (that is, `/wp-admin/index.php`), mouse over the **Pages** menu item on the left-hand side of the page and then click on **Add New** to create a new page. I usually name this page `Home`, as I use the blog directory as the first page that visitors see when visiting the site. From there, visitors can choose which blog they want to visit and are also shown a list of the most recent posts from each blog.

There's no need to enter any content on the page, unless you want to. The important part is selecting the **Blog Directory** template. Before you publish your new Home / blog directory page, make sure that you select **Blog Directory** as the **Template** value in the **Page Attributes** section. An example a Home / blog directory page can be seen in the following screenshot:

Example Home / blog directory page setup

Once you've got your page looking like the example, as shown in the previous screenshot, you can go ahead and publish that page. The **Update** button in the previous screenshot will say **Publish** if you've not yet published the page.

Next you'll want to set the newly created Home / blog directory page as the front page for the site. To do this, mouse over the **Settings** menu option on the left-hand side of the page and then click on **Reading**. For the **Front page displays** value, check **A static page (select below)**. Previously, **Your latest posts** was checked. Then for the **Front Page** drop-down menu, just select the **Home** page that we just created and click on the **Save Changes** button at the bottom of the page. I usually don't set anything for the **Posts page** drop-down menu because I never post to the "parent" site. If you do intend to make posts on the parent site, I'd suggest that you create a new blank page titled Posts and then select that page as your **Posts** page. The reading settings I use at multisite.longren.org can be as shown in the following screenshot:

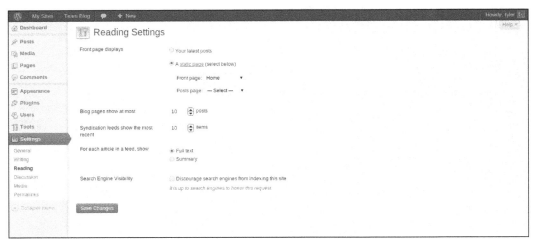

Reading settings setup

After you've saved your reading settings, open up your parent site in your browser and you should see something similar to what I showed in the *Blog directory example* screenshot. Again, there's no need for you to keep the exact setup that I've used in the example `blog-directory.php` file. You can give that any style/design that you want. You can rearrange the various pieces on the page as you prefer. You should probably have a decent working knowledge of HTML and CSS to accomplish this, however.

You should have a basic blog directory at this point. If you have any experience with PHP, HTML, and CSS, you can probably extend this basic code and do a whole lot more with it. The number of plugins is astounding and they are of very good quality, generally. And I think *Automattic* has done great things for WordPress in general. No other CMS can claim to have anything like the number of plugins that WordPress does.

Summary

You should be able to effectively manage themes and plugins in a multisite installation now. If you set the code up, you've got a directory showcasing network member content and, more importantly, know how to set up and customize a WordPress child theme now. In the next chapter, we'll be going over how you can let your users manage their own blogs. This includes using plugins and themes for creating and editing posts.

3
User Management and Permissions

When you're running a WordPress multisite installation, there's another user "level" that's not there on a normal, single site WordPress installation. This user is often referred to as the Super Administrator. The Super Admin is the user that you create when you first installed WordPress.

The Super Administrator

The Super Admin is the user who creates all the individual blogs and sites, administers theme availability for those individual sites, and is generally responsible for the health of the entire blog or site network. The Super Admin has many more right than typical users, even the administrator users for individual blogs or sites.

When you first login as the Super Admin, you'll see the WordPress **Dashboard** window just as you normally would. This dashboard is for the "root" site. Say your root site is `http://multisite.longren.org`, with individual blogs sitting at `http://multisite.longren.org/sydney/`. In the default **Dashboard** window the Super Admin will allow users to edit the contents of `http://multisite.longren.org/`. They can add pages, posts, and all the normal things you'd be able to do on a regular, single-site WordPress installation.

This default **Dashboard** window can be seen in the following screenshot:

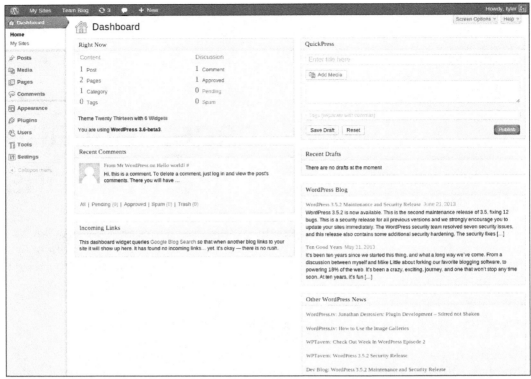

Initial Super Admin login dashboard

You probably won't want to do much on that initial **Dashboard** window. In the previous chapter, we used it to create our blog directory. That's all I ever use it for, so I rarely use that dashboard after the initial blog setup has been completed.

The Super Admin dashboard, or Network dashboard as I usually call it, is where all the fun happens. That's where we add new blogs, activate themes for use by individual blogs, activate plugins, and make network setup changes. The Network dashboard looks very similar to the regular dashboard, but with a few very big differences. Most of the differences you'll probably notice right away in the left-hand menu. The Network dashboard has options for **Sites**, **Users**, **Themes**, **Plugins**, **Settings**, and **Updates** in the left-hand navigation menu. Some of those navigation items exist on the regular dashboard, such as **Settings**, **Plugins**, and **Themes**, but **Sites** is totally unique to the Network dashboard. You can see the initial Network dashboard window in the following screenshot:

The initial Network dashboard

On the Network dashboard, there are quick links you can use to easily create a new site or create a new user. Under the **Right Now** heading, there are links that will allow you to create new sites and new users, or you can also search existing sites and users.

Regular blog or site administrators are treated just as they are in single-site WordPress installations, although there are some restrictions, such as plugin and theme installation. All these have to be done by the Super Admin. A regular blog or site administrator can create users for their individual sites, such as subscribers, authors, and editors.

When logged in as the Super Administrator, you can get an overview of the sites on your network by clicking on the **Sites** navigation item on the left-hand side of the Network dashboard. You'll be able to see the path of the site (that is, /tyler/, /sydney/, or /kayla/). It also allows you to see which users are assigned to which sites at a glance. You can see an example of this screen in the following screenshot:

Network dashboard site list

Management of users is also extremely easy from the Network dashboard. Clicking on the **Users** navigation item on the left-hand navigation bar will bring you to a page listing all the users in your network. An example can be seen in the following screenshot:

Network dashboard user list

Individual site management

The concept of the Super Administrator is a pretty simple thing to wrap your head around, so we're going to move onto letting individual blog or site owners manage their own sites, which isn't all that much different than in a single-site WordPress installation. The individual site dashboard will look just like a single-site WordPress dashboard, but you can see what it looks like in the following screenshot:

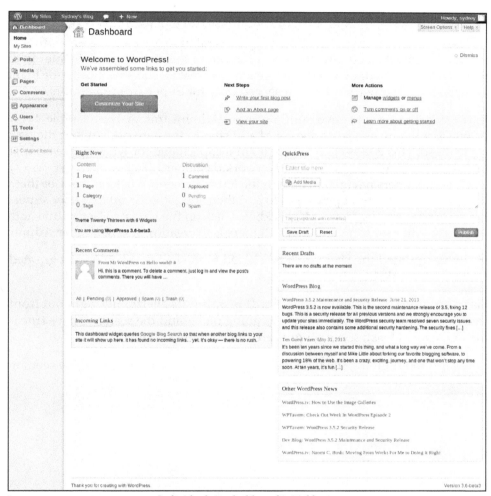

Individual site dashboard initial login

If my daughter Sydney wanted to log in to her blog dashboard, she would do so by visiting her blog URL and appending `/wp-admin/` to the end; so she'd end up at `http://multisite.longren.org/sydney/wp-admin/`, which you can see in the previous screenshot.

User roles and permissions

We've already covered most of the Super Admin information but this section will provide examples of user role permissions and various other role-based information.

Super Administrators can view and manage individual site dashboards. So I can log in as the Super Administrator and make posts, create pages, or set up sidebar widgets for Sydney.

If Sydney wanted to let a friend post on her blog, let's call her Bianca, she could do so just as she would on a single-site WordPress installation, by creating an Author user on her individual site (actually, there's a bit more to this that I'll explain later in this chapter). However, Sydney would not be able to create a site specifically for Bianca on the network. That permission is reserved only for Super Administrators.

In many cases it's useful to have multiple Super Administrators. For example, I could add Kayla as a Super Admin so she could add sites to the network without the need for me to do so. This is especially useful if I'm incapacitated for whatever reason. To add another Super Admin, go to your Network dashboard (/wp-admin/network/) and click on the **Users** navigation item in the left-side menu. Click on the user that you want to grant Super Admin privileges to and then check the **Grant this user super admin privileges for the Network** checkbox. Click on the **Update User** button at the bottom of the edit user form and that's all there is to creating another Super Admin.

After you've updated the user you'll be alerted to the fact that you've just granted another user a whole bunch of privileges.

This is part of the reason why I love WordPress. It puts everything right out front and makes admins well aware of what's going on behind the scenes. That's true of WordPress core at least; some plugins are not so transparent.

The message about giving the new user Super Admin permissions can be seen in the following screenshot:

Alert about Super Admin privileges

For reference, the following screenshot shows the exact setup for Kayla, making her a Super Admin. That screenshot was after I'd clicked the **Update User** button.

Additional Super Admin creation

There are quite a few user roles in WordPress, straight out of the box. The WordPress Codex does a great job of explaining this at `http://codex.wordpress.org/Roles_and_Capabilities`.

Obviously, there's the Super Admin and the regular site admin. We've discussed those roles in some depth already.

The **Editor** role is a person who can publish and edit the posts of other users but can also make posts of their own. When I was in the newspaper industry, our actual newspaper editor was assigned the Editor role in WordPress multisite so they could effectively edit the posts of everyone's individual blogs.

The **Author** role is someone who can publish and edit their own posts. Editors, Admins, and Super Admins all have the ability to modify or delete posts by Authors.

A **Contributor** is somebody who writes and creates their own posts but who has no ability to publish them. Any of the roles above a Contributor must publish their posts for them. Contributors are often accounts for guest bloggers or other non-regular bloggers.

The role with the least permission is the **Subscriber**. They can only manage their profile and make comments on posts, but only if that post has comments enabled.

Again, when I was in the newspaper industry, we had a large number of subscribers on a few, small-town newspaper sites. That was only due to the fact that we would require users to sign up and be logged in before they could read entire posts. It was free to sign up, so this was basically a way to measure the readership for each paper.

Requiring registration for the typical blog isn't going to go well, so I advise against it. The reason it works for newspapers is that newspapers deliver highly localized content that's not available elsewhere. People have gotten used to reading columns from their favorite columnists, and will gladly sign up so they can read their favorite reporter's or columnist's articles online. Not many industries can pull off the required registration, the newspaper industry being the only one that I can think of.

A lot of this hasn't been directly related to WordPress multisite but I think it's important that you have a good concept of the various user roles and what can and cannot be accomplished by users with those roles.

All users created at the Network dashboard level don't have the various roles under Admin available to them, since they're the Admin user for an individual site.

If Sydney wanted to add Bianca as an author to Sydney's blog, Kayla or I as Super Admins would have to first add a user for Bianca at the Network dashboard level. You'd do this from `/wp-admin/network/user-new.php`. You can see this in the following screenshot:

Add a regular network user

After the Super Admin has added Bianca, Sydney can log in to her dashboard and send Bianca a request to join her site. Sydney would click on the **Users** navigation item on the left-hand menu and then click on the **Add Existing** button at the top. I've highlighted that button in the following screenshot:

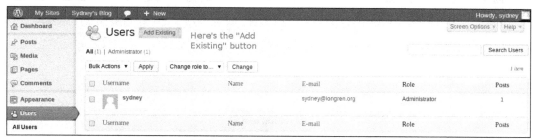

Add existing User Button location

Now you should be on a page titled **Add Existing User**. All Sydney has to do is enter Bianca's e-mail address and then choose a role for her. Sydney will want to select **Author** for the role so Bianca can write posts and publish them on her own.

The default role selected is **Subscriber**, so make sure you change the role if you want to allow the person to make posts. For reference you can refer to the following screenshot:

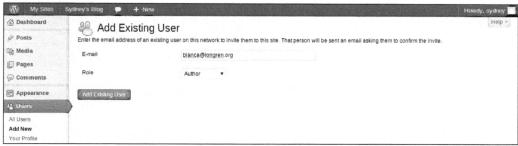

Add network user to individual site

Once you've clicked the **Add Existing User** button, an e-mail will be sent to that user asking them to confirm the invite; you're also notified of this before adding the user, and after actually adding the user. This is depicted in the following screenshot:

Invitation e-mail

Once Bianca receives the confirmation e-mail all she has to do is click the link to activate her account. Once she's clicked the link she can then log in at /sydney/ wp-admin/. Bianca would have received her password via e-mail after her network account was created by the Super Admin.

You can see an example of the confirmation e-mail received by Bianca following Sydney's request to add her to her site in the following screenshot:

Invitation e-mail sent to new user

After Bianca has logged in at Sydney's dashboard (/sydney/wp-admin) she can make and edit posts just as a normal, single-site WordPress author would do.

If you find yourself needing more control over user roles, there are a couple of plugins you should take a look at.

The first is **Members**. It is an extremely powerful tool. It's essentially a user, role, and content management plugin to enhance WordPress as a true CMS.

Members will let you create, edit, and delete roles. You can also define capabilities for those roles, which is extremely useful for complex organizations requiring very specific capabilities for a very small set of users. You can find Members at http://wordpress.org/plugins/members/. It supports WordPress multisite quite well.

Members is a very popular plugin. As of late June 2013, it's been downloaded over 214,000 times. It was created by *Justin Tadlock*, the guy behind themehybrid.com.

Refer to the following screenshot to see how capabilities are added to a role in Members. It's straight from the WordPress' plugin page.

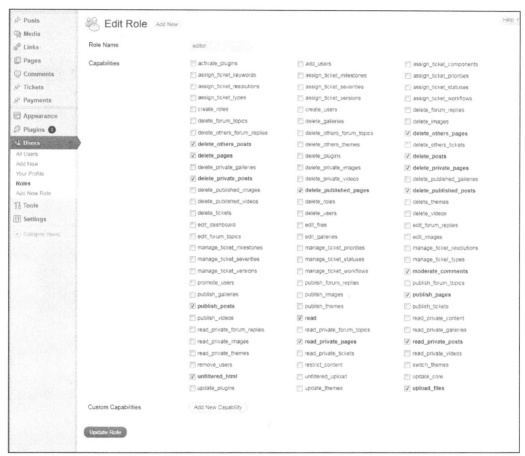

Members role capabilities

Another plugin, similar to Members, is called **User Role Editor**, and is also WordPress multisite friendly. It offers many of the same features offered by Members, but seems to be under more active development than Members. Members, at the moment of writing, hasn't been updated since December 4, 2012, while User Role Editor was just updated on May 24, 2013.

User Role Editor is also a very popular plugin with over 650,000 downloads, which is pretty impressive. I'm not certain, but I think Members has been around longer than User Role Editor, yet User Role Editor has over twice as many downloads.

The author of User Role Editor is *Vladimir Garagulya;* you can find his personal site at shinephp.com. He's got some really good content there. The following screenshot shows the User Role Editor capability management screen. You can compare that with the equivalent screen in Members from the previous screenshot and decide which interface you like better. Both should be pretty similar as far as functionality goes.

User Role Editor role capabilities

Summary

You should now have a pretty good understanding of all the different user roles and their permissions. The Super Admin is a really powerful user, so make sure you keep that password safe. In the next chapter, we'll discuss various ways that you can protect your site from the evils of the Internet.

4
Protecting Your
Multisite Network

Securing your WordPress installation is critical, whether on a single-site installation, or on multisite installations. WordPress is the most popular CMS right now, which means that a lot of hackers are targeting it simply due to the large number of users. People aren't always good about keeping their WordPress installations up-to-date, which makes the job of the hacker even easier.

Imagine, if you will, that you're running three blogs, and all are running as single-site WordPress installations. When a security update or other new version of WordPress is released, you'd have to do the upgrade on all three blogs.

Now, if you had those three blogs running off a WordPress multisite installation, you'd just need to do the upgrade once and be done with it. Same goes for updating plugins and themes as well. Do it once on the multisite network and the changes are applied across all network member sites. After updating, you should manually verify that the updates are applied by checking the individual sites. There may be conflicts with plugins or themes, because the plugins or themes on one site may not exist on another site.

Understanding the basics

There are some really basic things we can do right away when installing a new WordPress site to enhance its security.

It's often stated on the Internet that deleting `wp-admin/install.php` and `wp-admin/upgrade.php` is a good way to add security. That's not really true, though, as the files can't be accessed after an installation. However, that doesn't mean that you can't remove them. I usually remove those two files.

The next thing you should absolutely do is make the proper edits to `wp-config.php`. There's one thing in particular that you really need to do when setting up `wp-config.php`, and that is generating unique salts and keys used for authentication. The section in `wp-conifg` where this is defined can be seen in the following screenshot:

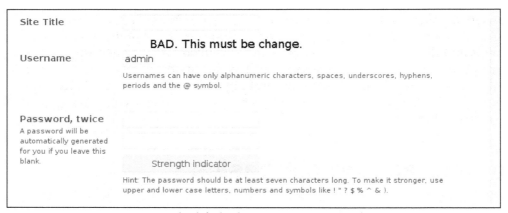

Unique salt and key setup

Another great thing you can do before you're even finished installing WordPress is to choose a username other than Admin. By default, the installation wizard chooses the `admin` username, as seen in the next screenshot. Everybody knows about this, so Internet evildoers have started to exploit this default username. They do so by running a brute-force password cracking attempt with `admin` as the username, and a lot, I mean a *lot* of password combinations. If there is no `admin` user, their work is pointless. So I highly suggest you choose something other than the `admin` username.

Site Title	
	BAD. This must be change.
Username	admin
	Usernames can have only alphanumeric characters, spaces, underscores, hyphens, periods and the @ symbol.
Password, twice A password will be automatically generated for you if you leave this blank.	
	Strength indicator
	Hint: The password should be at least seven characters long. To make it stronger, use upper and lower case letters, numbers and symbols like ! " ? $ % ^ &).

Using the default admin username is not good

Securing wp-admin

Some people like to set another password for accessing their `/wp-admin/` (Dashboard) page. And this is really easy to do if you're using Apache for your webserver. This will essentially have the effect of **double authentication**. You'll need to enter one username and password before you can even get to the page where you can enter your WordPress username and password. This is achieved by placing a file named `.htpasswd` (similar to `.htaccess`) inside your `/wp-admin/` folder. There are a lot of tools out there to generate the content of the `.htaccess` file for you. The one I use most frequently is developed by *Andreas Gehrke* and is simply called **HTPASSWD GENERATOR**. You can see a glimpse of it in the following screenshot:

HTPASSWD GENERATOR – CREATE HTPASSWD

Use the htpasswd generator to create passwords for htpasswd files.

Just enter username and password and an entry for a htpasswd file is generated. You can use the htacccess Authentication generator to create a htaccess file that will password protect your site or a directory. This htpasswd generator creates passwords that are hashed using the MD5 algorithm, which means that you can use it for sites hosted on any platform, including Windows and Linux. You can also create htpasswd passwords with PHP on your own server – this technique only works on Linux though. Read more about htpasswd files.

Username
Enter the username you would like to add to your `.htpasswd` file.

| tyler |

Password
Enter the password to be encrypted.

| ••••••• |

| Create .htpasswd file |

Learn more about htpasswd in the htpasswd article.

I do **NOT** log **ANY** data entered in this form.

Copyright © Andreas Gehrke | Design: Blog Design Studio

HTPASSWD GENERATOR

Just enter the username and password you want, and click on the **Create .htpasswd file** button. Andreas' tool will do its thing and spit out a text area control containing the content for you to put into your .htpasswd file. The page showing you the output from Andreas' tool can be seen in the following screenshot:

.htpasswd entry created
Copy the text below into your .htpasswd file.

Remember: One entry per line.

```
tyler:$apr1$Mx5CEONf$bEs7BlCPrEDzud3pGX6jh/
```

Learn more about htpasswd in the htpasswd article.

I do **NOT** log **ANY** data entered in this form.

Copyright © Andreas Gehrke | Design: Blog Design Studio

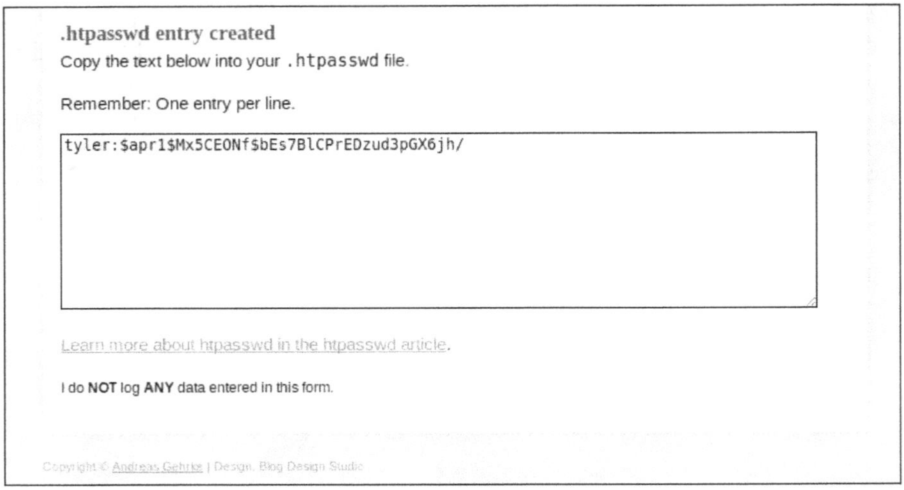

HTPASSWD GENERATOR results

Simply copy the contents (tyler: and everything following it) of the textarea as seen in the preceding screenshot and paste them into a blank file called .htpasswd. If you're using Windows XP, this may be impossible for you, because Windows XP will not allow files to start with a period. The easiest way to do this is to open your FTP client such as FileZilla, go to your wp-admin folder, right-click in the bottom-right panel (the one showing the files on your FTP server), and then click on **Create new file**. A window will open asking what the name of your new file should be. Enter .htpasswd and click on the **OK** button. The following screenshot was taken immediately after I right-clicked and selected **Create new file**:

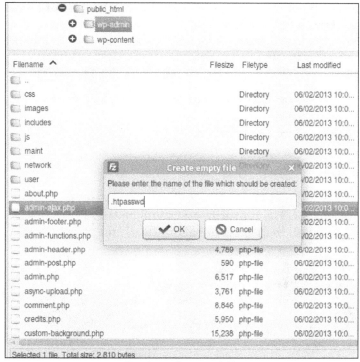

Creating a .htpasswd file

Once you've clicked on the **OK** button, you should now see the `.htpasswd` file in your `wp-admin` folder. You should repeat those steps and also create a blank file named `.htaccess` in your `wp-admin` folder; we'll need it later. Now, while still in FileZilla, right-click on the `.htpasswd` file and then click on **View/Edit**. This will open the file for editing and, when you save the file, FileZilla will ask if you want to re-upload the changed file.

Once the `.htpasswd` file is open in your text/code editor, enter the content from the textarea generated with the HTPASSWD GENERATOR tool. You can see what the content of my `.htpasswd` file looks like in the following screenshot:

Example .htpasswd content

There's one more step before we can start entering our first set of login credentials. Still in FileZilla, view/edit the file named .htaccess in your wp-admin folder. You'll need to edit the first line of the following code to point to the location your .htpasswd file sits at. For me, it's in /srv/www/multisite.longren.org/public_content/wp-admin/.

AuthUserFile /srv/www/multisite.longren.org/public_content/wp-admin/. htpasswd

AuthName "Authorization Required"

AuthType Basic

require valid-user

Your .htaccess file sitting in your wp-admin folder should look similar to what's in the following screenshot. The only difference will be the AuthUserFile line, which will have a different path than mine but should still end in /wp-admin/.htpasswd.

Example .htaccess content

Securing the wp-includes folder

You can secure your wp-includes folder too. None of the scripts in that folder have any reason to be accessed by any user. One method to restrict access to the wp-includes scripts is to use the mod_rewrite Apache module. The following code is taken from the *WordPress Codex*; it's what I always use in the .htaccess file in the root of my websites. Edit your main .htaccess file as we did before with FileZilla. The "main" .htaccess file is the one that sits in the root of your web doc's folder, or where you see the wp-config.php file. Enter the following code immediately before the #BEGIN WordPress line or immediately after the #END WordPress line.

```
# Block the include-only files.
RewriteEngine On
RewriteBase /
RewriteRule ^wp-admin/includes/ - [F,L]
RewriteRule !^wp-includes/ - [S=3]
RewriteRule ^wp-includes/js/tinymce/langs/.+\.php - [F,L]
RewriteRule ^wp-includes/theme-compat/ - [F,L]
```

Once you've added that code to your main .htaccess file, save it and re-upload it to your server with FileZilla. After you've added that code to your main .htaccess file, it should look something like what you see in the following screenshot:

```
1   RewriteEngine On
2   RewriteBase /
3   RewriteRule ^wp-admin/includes/ - [F,L]
4   RewriteRule !^wp-includes/ - [S=3]
5   RewriteRule ^wp-includes/js/tinymce/langs/.+\.php - [F,L]
6   RewriteRule ^wp-includes/theme-compat/ - [F,L]
7
8   # BEGIN WordPress
9   <IfModule mod_rewrite.c>
10  RewriteEngine On
11  RewriteBase /
12  RewriteRule ^index\.php$ - [L]
13  RewriteRule ^wp-svbtle/ /wp-content/plugins/wp-svbtle-editor/ [QSA,L]
14  RewriteCond %{REQUEST_FILENAME} !-f
15  RewriteCond %{REQUEST_FILENAME} !-d
16  RewriteRule . /index.php [L]
17  </IfModule>
18
19  # END WordPress
20  |
```

Final .htaccess after securing wp-includes

Securing wp-config.php

Making sure that wp-config is secure is pretty simple. The only people who should have access to the file are you and the user your web server runs as.

Sometimes, for whatever reason, people will try to surf to your wp-config.php file. Won't do them much good in most cases, but there's another .htaccess trick we can employ to ensure that they're not allowed to get to wp-config.php. The following code is what's needed to deny access to wp-config.php:

```
<files wp-config.php>
order allow,deny
deny from all
</files>
```

You'll need to add the preceding code to your main `.htaccess` file, the one sitting in the same folder as `wp-config.php`. So, using FileZilla again, view/edit the main `.htaccess` file and add the preceding code to it. The following screenshot shows what your `.htaccess` file should look like with the preceding code added:

```
<files wp-config.php>
order allow,deny
deny from all
</files>

RewriteEngine On
RewriteBase /
RewriteRule ^wp-admin/includes/ - [F,L]
RewriteRule !^wp-includes/ - [S=3]
RewriteRule ^wp-includes/js/tinymce/langs/.+\.php - [F,L]
RewriteRule ^wp-includes/theme-compat/ - [F,L]

# BEGIN WordPress
<IfModule mod_rewrite.c>
RewriteEngine On
RewriteBase /
RewriteRule ^index\.php$ - [L]
RewriteRule ^wp-svbtle/ /wp-content/plugins/wp-svbtle-editor/ [QSA,L]
RewriteCond %{REQUEST_FILENAME} !-f
RewriteCond %{REQUEST_FILENAME} !-d
RewriteRule . /index.php [L]
</IfModule>

# END WordPress
```

Restrict access to wp-config.php

Security through obscurity

This isn't a great strategy for system security. We've already done some "security through obscuring" things, such as renaming the `admin` account to something else.

Another way we can make use of security through obscurity is to change the database table prefixes. By default, WordPress database tables have the `wp_` prefix. The database table prefix is set in `wp-config.php`. Changing the database table prefix can be a real pain if you do it after you've installed WordPress. It's always a good idea to decide what table prefix you'd like to use before beginning with the WordPress installation.

For this, we're going to assume we're starting off with a fresh WordPress multisite install. Rename `wp-config-sample.php` to `wp-config.php`. Open it up and set all your database connection settings and everything, just as we talked about in the *Configuring the WordPress multisite feature* section in *Chapter 1, Getting Started with WordPress Multisite*.

Now look for the line that starts with `$table_prefix = 'wp_';`. It's generally right below the section of `wp-config` where we generate our authentication unique keys and salts. The following screenshot shows you what the line that you need to edit looks like:

```
64
65  /**
66   * WordPress Database Table prefix.
67   *
68   * You can have multiple installations in one database if you give each a unique
69   * prefix. Only numbers, letters, and underscores please!
70   */
71  $table_prefix  = 'wp_';
72
```

Where to change the table prefix

I'd say that the vast majority of people use the default table prefix. I even use it on many of my sites. This could pose a problem though if a serious WordPress vulnerability were discovered. The attackers would know the exact table names and where all the data is if the WordPress site is using the default `wp_` table prefix.

By using something other than the default table prefix, those attackers would have no idea what our table naming structure is. They'd know that we have tables with names such as `*_options`, `*_posts`, and `*_users`, but they'd have no clue as to what should replace the `*`. So they would effectively be unable to do any damage to our site if it's not using the default database table prefix. I like to use totally random table prefixes. Something resembling what you can see in the following screenshot:

```
64
65  /**
66   * WordPress Database Table prefix.
67   *
68   * You can have multiple installations in one database if you give each a unique
69   * prefix. Only numbers, letters, and underscores please!
70   */
71  $table_prefix  = 'crazyhackerskeepout_';
72
```

A custom table prefix

As you can see from the preceding screenshot, I chose to use the `crazyhackerskeepout_` table prefix. That's legible, but you can even use absolutely, totally random characters. Your table prefix could consist of just random letters and numbers, something like `a34kasd93`.

Security through obscurity only really applies to two WordPress situations: changing the default administrator username and using something other than the default database table prefix.

Backups

Backup, backup, backup! I know it's boring, and sometimes tedious, but it's something you *must* do. There's one plugin that I've been using for a while now on all of my WordPress sites to take care of backups. The plugin is called **BackWPup** and is free in the WordPress Plugin Directory. You can find the page at http:// wordpress.org/plugins/backwpup/.

BackWPup is very powerful. It takes care of backing up individual files, such as themes and plugin files, and also creates backups of your database.

The thing that I really, really like about BackWPup is that it integrates with remote storage environments, such as Dropbox, Amazon S3, and regular FTP. I've got all my WordPress sites set up to do weekly backups of files and the database, and then send that backup file to a folder in my Dropbox account. It works awesomely well, and is a really valuable tool. In the following screenshot you can see how to create a new BackWPup job, telling it what to include in the backup:

BackWPup creating a backup job

Summary

By now, you should have a very secure WordPress multisite setup. I really suggest that you implement everything covered, most of them only take a few minutes to implement. I don't think a single one takes much longer than 15 minutes, even for a beginner.

In the next chapter, we'll be going over how to bring multiple, standard WordPress blogs into a single WordPress multisite network of blogs. This will be particularly useful if you run more than one WordPress site and would like to be able to manage them from a single dashboard.

5
Migrating Multiple WordPress Blogs to a Multisite Network

WordPress multisite is a very attractive solution for individuals who manage multiple individual WordPress blogs. Bringing those individual blogs into one WordPress multisite network would be ideal, allowing the administrator to administer all blogs from one location, the Network dashboard.

The process of moving a standalone WordPress blog into a multisite network sounds as if it could be quite an undertaking but it's actually not that scary process.

In this chapter, I'll be using my `longren.org` blog as an example of a standalone WordPress site that we want to move to `multisite.longren.org/tlongren/`.

Before you do anything, I suggest you make multiple backups. Back up the standalone blog and back up the multisite network you're importing the standalone blog into. Just back everything up, please.

Exporting your standalone blog content

First we need to export our content from our standalone blog, which is really simple to do in WordPress. While logged into your standalone blog **Dashboard** window, click on the **Tools** left-side menu option, and then click on the **Import** menu item. This will bring you to a screen titled **Export**, with a little hammer and screwdriver icon next to the **Export** page title. You can see what this screen should look like in the following screenshot:

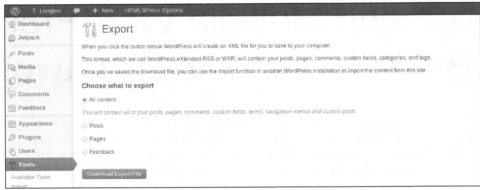

Content Export screen

On the **Export** screen, we have a few options regarding which kind of data we'd like to export. We can export **All content**, only **Posts**, only **Pages**, or only **Feedback**. As shown in the preceding screenshot, we're going to export **All content**, as you see it is checked. Any custom post types that you have will also be exported.

Once you've selected **All Content** to export, just click on the blue **Download Export File** button. That will cause WordPress to generate a .wxr file that we can then later import into our WordPress multisite network. After you've clicked on the blue **Download Export File** button, you'll be prompted to download a .xml file from your browser. That .xml file is essentially your .wxr file.

Save that .xml file to your desktop or somewhere you can access it quickly. We'll need it in a little bit when we move back over to the WordPress multisite dashboard to re-import this xml/wxr file. The name of the export file will be something similar to tlongren.wordpress.2013-07-12.xml. The export files can become quite large depending on what kind of content your blog has. For example, tlongren. wordpress.2013-07-12.xml is 15.5 MB.

It's a good idea to make sure that all of your data is actually contained in the export file. What I typically do, is open the export file (the .xml file, the one on your desktop) in a regular text editor (Sublime Text 3 is my favorite). When you've got the export file open in your text editor, look at the last line of the file. If the line is the most recent post you've made to your standalone blog, you should be good to go. If it isn't your most recent post, something may have gone wrong. This will happen often when you have a huge WordPress database, in which case you'll need to do some more customized work to get a proper export file.

In the following screenshot, you can see the contents of my tlongren. wordpress.2013-07-12.xml file, and you can see that the last XML entry is for a post titled **HTML5Press Needs a New Name**. Well, that just happens to be that last post (http://www.longren.org/html5press-needs-a-new-name/) I made before running the .wxr file export from my standalone WordPress site.

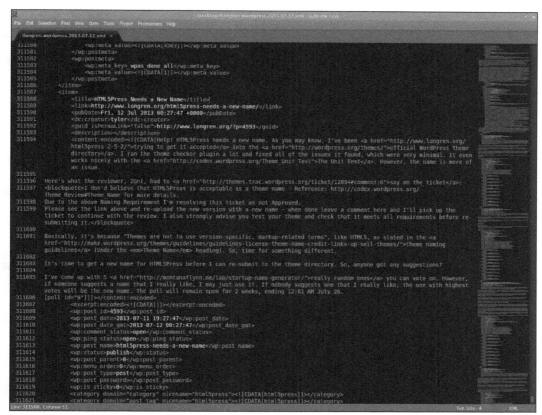

Export file contents

It's also worth noting that some plugins can interfere with the export creation process, resulting in an entirely empty export file. If you do end up with an empty export file, I suggest disabling all of your plugins and then running the export again.

It's also a good idea to delete all of the spam comments before you do the export, otherwise you'll end up with a ton of spam comments in your export file, potentially making it much, much larger than it normally would be.

To delete all of your spam comments from your standalone blog, go to your **Dashboard** and click on the **Comments** menu item on the left-hand menu. Then, click on the **Spam** link at the top of the page titled **Comments**. It has a number in parentheses indicating how many spam comments there are. As you can see in the following screenshot, I've got **1,093** spam comments just sitting there waiting to be deleted.

Spam comments location

Now to delete those comments, click on the **Spam** link referenced in the preceding screenshot and you'll be brought to a page listing nothing but your spam comments. It will have an **Empty Spam** button on it, as you can see in the following screenshot. Clicking on that **Empty Spam** button will clear all of the spam comments out of your standalone WordPress database, meaning they won't be included in your export file.

Empty Spam button

So now you should have an export file, in .xml format, even though the WordPress folks refer to it as a .wxr file. Now, it's time to bring this export file into your multisite network.

Importing standalone content to a specific network blog

I'm going to bring the .xml export file from my standalone WordPress blog into my *Tyler* blog, which is available at http://multisite.longren.org/tyler/. To do this, login to your multisite dashboard (http://multisite.longren.org/wp-admin/) and then mouse over the **My Sites** menu item in the top-left of the screen. Then mouse over the blog that you want to import into, **Tyler's Blog** in this case, and then click on **Dashboard** to get the dashboard for the network blog you want to import the export data into. Have a look at the following screenshot to see exactly what I'm talking about:

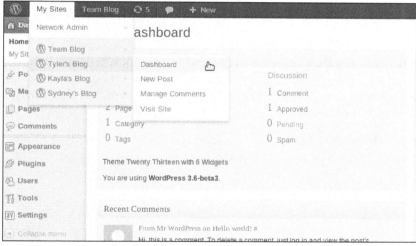

Go to dashboard of the blog to import into

Now you should be at the dashboard for the network blog that you're importing the data into. Since we're using my blog as an example here, you should now be at the **Tyler's Blog** dashboard, rather than the Network dashboard. You can see the dashboard for **Tyler's Blog** in the following screenshot:

Dashboard for Network blog we're importing into

Now you'll need to install a plugin so we can import our export file into **Tyler's Blog**. This is one thing that has always bugged me about WordPress. I have no idea why the plugin that is needed to import the export files isn't built into the core of WordPress, instead of being a standalone plugin. But I'm not on the WordPress team, so I'm sure they have their reasons that I'm not privy to.

So, from the **Tyler's Blog** dashboard, click on the **Tools** item on the left-hand side menu and then click on **Import**, as seen in the following screenshot:

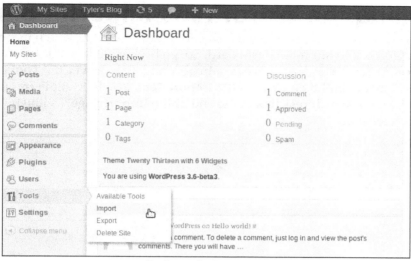

Getting to the Import area

When you get to the **Import** page you'll be presented with a bunch of options but we only care about the last option, **WordPress**, that informs us that we must install a plugin. All the other options are for importing into WordPress from other blogging platforms or another CMS. You can choose to make use of those if you wish but those other options are outside the scope of this book.

You can see the **Import** screen that lists all the import options in the following screenshot:

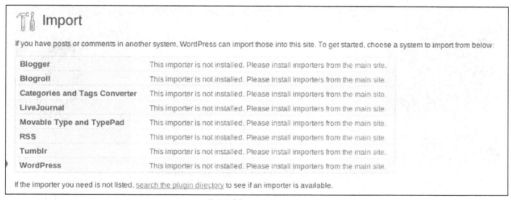

Initial Import screen

Installing the WordPress Importer plugin

Now we need to install the plugin to be able to import our data, which means we have to go back to our main dashboard. So, go back to your main dashboard (`http://multisite.longren.org/wp-admin/`), and mouse over the **Tools** item in the left-hand menu, and then click on the **Import** item. You'll be at the **Import** page again. Click on the **WordPress** link at the end of the **Import** page, as illustrated in the following screenshot:

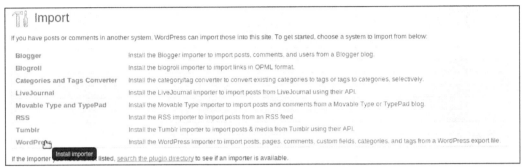

Click to install WordPress Importer

After clicking on the **WordPress** item, a modal window will appear with a big red **Install Now** button in the top-right corner of the modal window. You can see an illustration of the modal window in the following screenshot. Just click on the **Install Now** button to install the plugin. It should just install automatically.

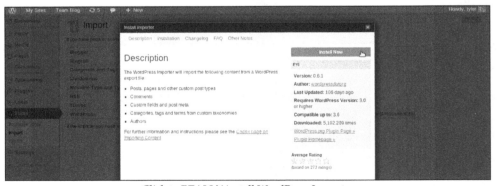

Click to REALLY install WordPress Importer

Now, this method may not work for everyone, like me. If you click the red **Install Now** button and you see a screen like what you see in the following screenshot, you'll need to manually install the plugin, which is easier than it sounds.

Hostname

FTP Username

FTP Password

Connection Type   ● FTP ○ FTPS (SSL)

This means manual plugin installation needed

If you see a screen like the previous screenshot you'll need to install the plugin manually. It's really quite simple. First, download the plugin from its page on the WordPress Plugin Directory. You can find it at `http://wordpress.org/plugins/wordpress-importer/`. Just click on the big red Download Version x.x.x button to download the plugin's ZIP file. You can see an example of the plugin's page on the WordPress Plugin Directory in the following screenshot:

WordPress Plugin Directory Importer plugin download page

Once you've downloaded the `.zip` file, named something similar to `wordpress-importer.0.6.1.zip`, open it up and extract the `wordpress-importer` folder to your desktop. Then, open FileZilla and upload it to your `wp-content/plugins` folder. By this point, you should be more than comfortable using FileZilla to upload files to your WordPress multisite installation.

After you've uploaded the importer plugin folder, go to your Network dashboard (`http://multisite.longren.org/wp-admin/network/`) and just click on the **Plugins** menu item in the left-side menu. Scroll down the page a bit and you should see a plugin named **WordPress Importer**. That's the plugin you just installed, either automatically or via FTP upload. To enable it, click on the **Network Activate** link directly under the **WordPress Importer** name, as seen in the following screenshot:

Network-activate the WordPress Importer plugin

Now that the importer plugin is available for our network sites, we need to go back to **Tyler's Blog** dashboard, just as we did earlier. Once there, mouse over the **Tools** item in the left-side menu and then click on **Import**, pretty much as we did earlier in the chapter. Except this time, there'll be a **WordPress** link in blue that wasn't there before we network-activated the WordPress Importer plugin. You can see this new **WordPress** link in the following screenshot:

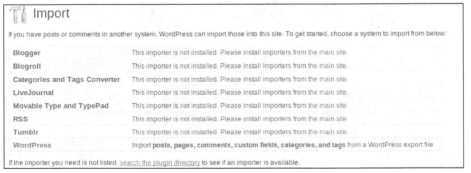

WordPress Importer now available to use

Importing content to the network site

Now that the WordPress Importer plugin is ready to go, just click on the blue **WordPress** link as seen in the previous screenshot. After clicking on that blue **WordPress** link you'll be taken to the **Import WordPress** page. You can see it in the following screenshot:

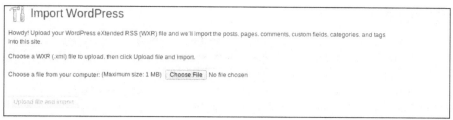
Import WordPress screen

Now here's the good stuff. You'll notice the **Choose File** form button in the previous screenshot. Click on that button, it will open up and let you select a file from your computer. Navigate to wherever your `.xml` (`.wxr`) file is and double-click that file.

After you've selected your file, the **Upload file and import** button is activated, just as you can see in the following screenshot:

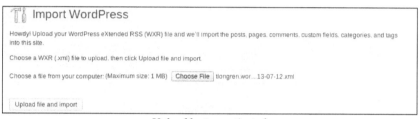
Upload button activated

Now all you have to do is click on the **Upload file and import** button and all the content from your standalone WordPress blog will be imported to your multisite network blog. Like magic!

There are a couple of things you need to take into consideration though; mostly themes and plugins. Some plugins you were using on your standalone WordPress blog may not be compatible with WordPress multisite.

Moving your content is one thing but you must also take into consideration the themes and plugins that you use. It's a fairly safe bet that you can just take all the theme folders from your standalone WordPress install and upload them to your WordPress multisite installation and network activate them.

That may not be the case with plugins, though, as some won't work with WordPress multisite. Most themes seem to play nicely with WordPress multisite.

Summary

By now, you should have all of the content and even themes and plugins from your standalone WordPress installation brought over into your shiny new WordPress multisite installation. In the next chapter, we'll be covering optimization of your WordPress multisite installation, various forms of caching, using a CDN, and minimizing some of your JavaScript and CSS files.

6
Site Optimization

Most people think of caching when speaking in the context of web development. And they should. There are so many different kinds of caching out there. There's client-side caching, server-side caching, and then there are Content Delivery Networks (CDN).

Client-side caching

We'll start off with client-side caching, because it's the easiest to understand and you're probably already fairly familiar with it. There's no doubt that at some point someone has asked you to—clear your cache. When someone says that, they're referring to your web browser's cache. Every web browser has some method for clearing the cache.

Often, client-side caching is defined via special `meta` tags in your website's HTML or via a special module for the Apache web server. Both cases control caching with the Cache-Control HTTP Headers.

Since client-side caching isn't really within the scope of this book, I'd like to move on to server-side caching. If you want to learn more about client-side caching, I suggest reading *Caching Tutorial for Web Authors and Webmasters*; it is available at the following link:

```
http://www.mnot.net/cache_docs/#CACHE-CONTROL
```

Server-side caching

Server-side caching is a lot more interesting than client-side, at least for me. Server-side caching saves content such as images, HTML, and CSS on the server that's hosting the website, as opposed to storing it in visitors browsers. With the server-side caching, the software doing the caching will check if there's a cached version of the current page before sending it to the browser for rendering. There's a plethora of WordPress plugins that offer various caching features.

Full-featured server-side caching plugins

One of the most popular caching plugins for WordPress is **W3 Total Cache**. I attribute its popularity to its rich feature set. It does a lot, from minifying your JavaScript and CSS code, to integrating seamlessly with paid CDNs. W3 Total Cache is a complex plugin and a little difficult to figure out at first.

I've never used W3 Total Cache, it's always seemed to be a bit of an overkill for most of my websites. If you are interested in more details about W3 Total Cache, check out the blog post by *Tom Dupuis*; it is available at the following link:

```
http://www.onlinemediamasters.com/w3-total-cache-settings/
```

Another popular plugin is called **WP Super Cache**. I used this plugin for a number of years and was very pleased with it. It's much more simple to configure than W3 Total Cache but doesn't lack all that many features.

W3 Total Cache and WP Super Cache are a couple of the most popular plugins available; combined, they have about 4 million downloads. W3 Total Cache is considered to be a WordPress performance optimization framework, while WP Super Cache is more of a tool for particular caching layers.

Hyper Cache is another immensely popular caching plugin for WordPress, one that I used up until about two months ago when I switched webhosts and got my own VPS. I think Hyper Cache is the easiest of the three plugins I've mentioned to use and configure.

Lite Cache setup

I hear you asking, "But which caching plugin are you currently using?". I'm now using a plugin called **Lite Cache**. Since this is the plugin I am currently most familiar with, I'll go into a little more detail on how to set it up properly.

First, download and network-activate the plugin, which you should know how to do by this point. I'm going to enable Lite Cache for **Tyler's Blog**, so from your main dashboard (`/wp-admin/`), mouse over **My Sites** in the top-left of the screen, then mouse over the blog you want to enable Lite Cache on, and then click on the **Dashboard** submenu item. Since, we network-activated this plugin, we don't have to activate it on the individual blog.

So, mouse over the **Tools** menu item in the left-hand menu, and then click on **Lite Cache**. Doing so will take you to the Lite Cache **Settings** page. It might even have some scary looking errors, like those seen in the following screenshot. If you don't see these errors, then you should be set. These errors happen on sites where the web server user doesn't have write access to the document root of the website. And this is fairly common and basically the worst-case-scenario with this plugin, so I think it's important to describe in detail what's going on and how to overcome possible issues.

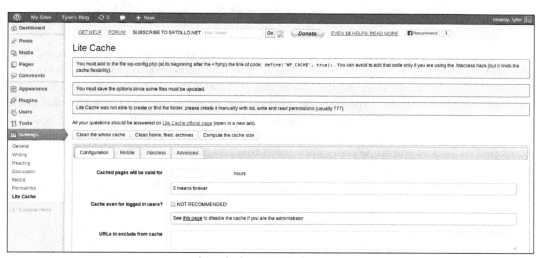

Scary looking Lite Cache errors

The first error shown in the preceding screenshot states that we must add a line of code to our `wp-config.php` file. Go ahead and open FileZilla, connect to your site, right-click on the `wp-config.php` file, and click on **View/Edit**. This will open `wp-config.php` for editing. I usually add the code immediately after the `<?php` part at the very top of the file. The line of code we need to add is as follows:

```
define('WP_CACHE', true);
```

After you've added that code, `wp-config.php` should look something like you see in the following screenshot:

```
   wp-config.php
 1   <?php
 2   define('WP_CACHE', true);
 3   /**
 4    * The base configurations of the WordPress.
 5    *
 6    * This file has the following configurations: MySQL settings, Table Prefix,
 7    * Secret Keys, WordPress Language, and ABSPATH. You can find more information
 8    * by visiting {@link http://codex.wordpress.org/Editing_wp-config.php Editing
 9    * wp-config.php} Codex page. You can get the MySQL settings from your web host.
10    *
11    * This file is used by the wp-config.php creation script during the
12    * installation. You don't have to use the web site, you can just copy this file
13    * to "wp-config.php" and fill in the values.
14    *
15    * @package WordPress
16    */
17
18   // ** MySQL settings - You can get this info from your web host ** //
19   /** The name of the database for WordPress */
20   define('DB_NAME', 'multisite');
21
```

wp-config.php after defining WP_CACHE

Save `wp-config.php` and FileZilla should ask if you want to upload the changed file, and you should let it. Now that we have that first error taken care of, let's check the Lite Cache **Settings** page again. Since you still have the **Settings** page open, just click on the **Save** button at the bottom. The second error mentioned is **You must save the options since some files must be updated.**, so saving the settings seems logical. After clicking on that **Save** button, we get more errors. The following screenshot looks just as bad as the first screenshot from this chapter:

More scary looking Lite Cache errors

The first error there again says **You must save the options since some files must be updated.**. This error will never go away until you create an `advanced-cache.php` file, located at `wp-content/advanced-cache.php`. Back in FileZilla, navigate to the `wp-content` folder for your WordPress install. Right-click anywhere in the bottom-right pane and then click on **Create new file**. A dialog box will pop up asking what you'd like the file to be named. Enter `advanced-cache.php` and then click on the **OK** button to create the file. You can see an example in the following screenshot:

Creating a file with FileZilla

Now, if you refresh the Lite Cache **Settings** page, it should look like what you see in the following screenshot, with just one error that states **Lite Cache was not able to create or find the folder, please create it manually with list, write and read permissions (usually 777)..** The folder that error mentions is the `wp-content/cache` folder.

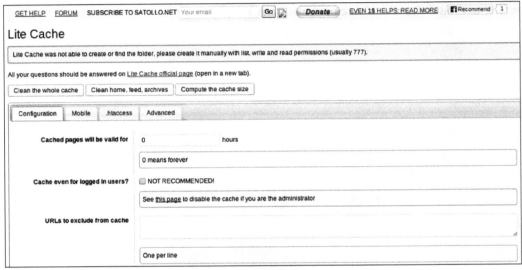

Last error in Lite Cache setup

The cache folder is where Lite Cache stores all of the static HTML cache files that it generates. In fact, the `wp-content/cache` folder is where most caching plugins store their data. For example, I've used Hyper Cache recently at `http://www.longren.org` and recently changed to Lite Cache. As you can see in the following screenshot, the `wp-content/cache/` folder contains plugin-specific folders, such as `hyper-cache` and `lite-cache`.

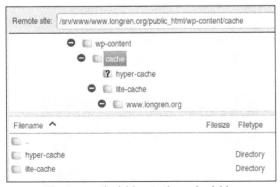

Plugin specific folders in the cache folder

To create the `wp-content/cache` folder, we'll do basically the same thing we did to create `wp-content/advanced-cache.php`, but will be creating a folder instead of an individual file. So, back in FileZilla, right-click anywhere in the remote directory listing pane (the bottom-right pane) and click on **Create directory**. Another pop-up window will appear asking what you'd like the name of your new folder to be, and will probably be prefixed by the full pathname. Just replace `New directory` with `cache`, as illustrated in the following screenshot. Then click on the **OK** button to actually create the `cache` folder.

Create the cache folder

Generally, the permissions on the `wp-content/cache` folder need to be pretty liberal. Most plugins suggest that you change the permissions to 777, which we can do with FileZilla.

So, still in FileZilla, right-click on your newly created `cache` folder and then click on **File permissions**. A pop-up window will appear titled **Change file attributes**; it has a bunch of checkboxes. To set the permissions for the `wp-content/cache` folder, you can either check all nine checkboxes, or you can enter `777` for the **Numeric value** field. The following screenshot shows how the **Change file attributes** window should look before clicking on the **OK** button.

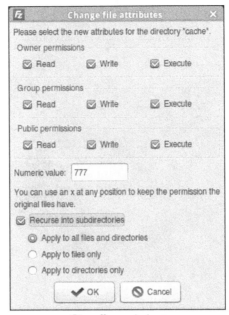

Give all permissions

After you've clicked on **OK** to set the permissions on the `cache` folder, go back to your web browser and to the Lite Cache **Settings** page. Now, you should have no errors, hopefully. I can't anticipate all scenarios, so there may be some rare, very specific circumstance that will prevent this from working. For example, if your webhost, for some reason, doesn't allow you to set file permissions.

To enable Lite Cache, just click on the **Save** button at the bottom of the page, as shown in the following screenshot:

Lite Cache settings with no errors!

But wait! There's another error, possibly. If you do see an error after saving that last time, it probably says **Unable to write the wp-content/advanced-cache.php file. Check the file or folder permissions..** The following screenshot demonstrates the error:

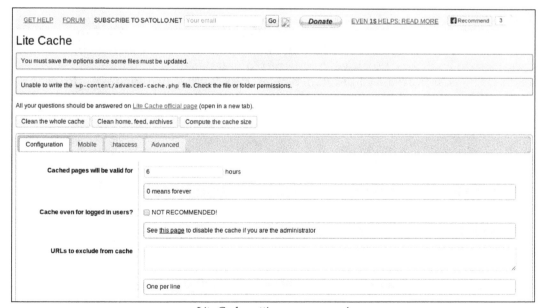

Lite Cache settings, more errors!

This is an easy fix though. Back in FileZilla, make sure you're in the `wp-content` folder for your WordPress multisite installation. In the remote file list pane in FileZilla (bottom-right pane), right-click on `advanced-cache.php` and click on **File permissions...**. Set the permissions to `777` as we did earlier, and then click on the **OK** button.

Now, we should be good to go with Lite Cache. Go back to the Lite Cache **Settings** page and click on the **Save** button at the bottom.

That's all I do to set up Lite Cache. I'm sure there are more advanced things you could do but this will get you a reliable, fast, but basic cache. Also, all the plugins I've mentioned are available for download in the official WordPress Plugin Directory, located at `http://wordpress.org/plugins/`.

CDNs and CloudFlare

I use CloudFlare for caching and security purposes but I just use the free plan. The free plan is awesome and I think everyone should use it. You don't even need to use CloudFlare as a CDN, but you can use it as a central place to manage DNS for all of your registered domain names.

CloudFlare acts as a reverse proxy for your website, according to the post on the *CloudFlare* blog that is available at `http://blog.cloudflare.com/top-tips-for-new-cloudflare-users`. They even have a WordPress plugin to make capturing visitors' real IP addresses easy and to tap into Akismet for not allowing known spammers to load your site. If you're interested in more about CloudFlare, I suggest reading this post from the CloudFlare blog as well. It even mentions WordPress integration.

CloudFlare gives really cool stats too; see an example in the following screenshot:

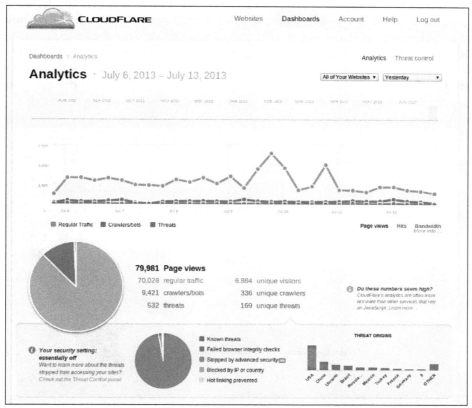

Cool CloudFlare stats

I have to suggest that everyone use the Jetpack plugin from Automattic as well. With that plugin, there is a module called Photon. Photon essentially makes copies of your images from posts and pages at `wordpress.com` and serves them on your blog from `wordpress.com`, reducing calls to your web server.

If you'd rather stay away from Jetpack to go the minimal route, you'll definitely want to check out *Cloudinary* at http://cloudinary.com/. Cloudinary is strictly an image management CDN. They have a free plan that would work well for most websites, but sites with more traffic would need a paid subscription. The free plan gives you 500 MB of storage, a 50,000 image limit, and 1 GB of bandwidth per month. All you do is upload your image, click on it after upload, and reference the image URL provided by Cloudinary in your post or page, instead of referencing the image on your server. You can see an example of Cloudinary in the following screenshot:

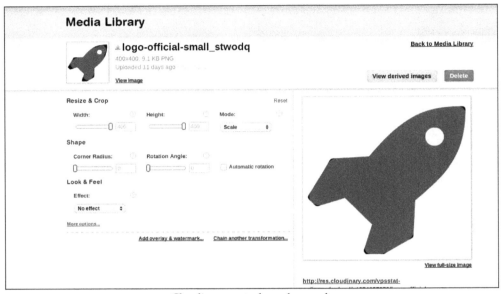

Cloudinary control panel example

If you're comfortable editing PHP files, another great option for making use of a CDN is http://cdnjs.com. If you're using, for example, a plugin or theme that uses jQuery UI, you could replace the default call to the .js file with the corresponding URL at *cdnjs*.

Summary

You should have a pretty fast website at this point. The server-side caching alone makes an amazing difference, as does CloudFlare. I am still amazed at the number of features CloudFlare is able to offer in their free service.

In the next chapter, we'll be discussing troubleshooting common problems related to WordPress multisite. We'll also cover maintenance of your site such as installing updates and ensuring that your site is always available.

7
Troubleshooting and Maintaining Stability

We'll go through some common WordPress multisite issues and how to troubleshoot them. Some of the most common issues I've encountered involve the site structure, whether it's a directory-based installation or an installation using subdomains.

If you're using a directory-based installation, as we used earlier in the book and as I'm using at `http://multisite.longren.org`, and you're encountering odd problems such as your sites just not working, it's likely an issue with the `.htaccess` file. This could include your individual blogs not loading at all, or maybe they'll load but won't have any styling applied to them.

If you're using a subdomain-based installation, you'll need to make sure that your web server has the domains all setup in Apache, however that may be done on your particular server. It varies from webhost to webhost and from Linux distribution to distribution. Subdomain sites use wildcard domain records, so be sure that your domain has a wildcard subdomain added. Basically, add an **A** record to your DNS records; where you'd normally put the subdomain name, put an asterisk symbol. If you're using CloudFlare to manage your DNS, the following screenshot shows a wildcard subdomain setup for the `longren.org` domain. Adding a wildcard is like having infinite subdomains. Without it, you'd need to create a new subdomain for each network site.

Wildcard subdomain on CloudFlare

In the preceding screenshot, you can see the wildcard DNS record; the IP listed is the IP hosting `longren.org`, so make sure that yours is set to whatever IP is hosting your domain. In most cases, it's probably the same IP that your www **A** record is pointing to.

Backups

I like to use the **BackWPup** plugin for taking care of backups. I especially like it because it makes backing up to Dropbox really easy. It's available for free in the WordPress plugin at `http://wordpress.org/plugins/backwpup/`. I've used it for all my personal sites as well as for customers. It makes scheduling backups really easy too.

You'll want to use BackWPup from the **Network Admin** side of the **Dashboard** window, instead of on individual blogs. The backup creation screen can be seen in the following screenshot.

BackWPup also comes in a pro version that adds some features such as the ability to use custom API keys for Dropbox and SugarSync, backing up job settings, the system testing wizard, and other features. The free version has been sufficient for most of my needs, but some of the pro features would be nice to have for certain sites. BackWPup is a good backup solution because it will backup your database and will also backup your files.

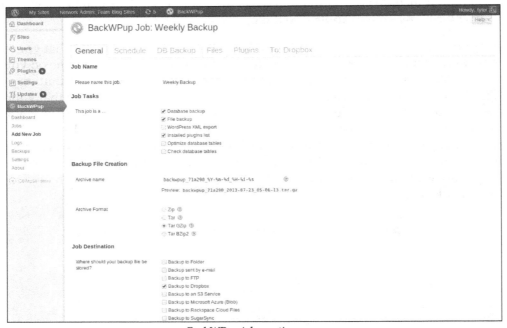

BackWPup job creation page

Updating the WordPress core

Sometimes, for whatever reason, you have to manually upgrade the WordPress core to versions, such as from Version 3.5.2 to Version 3.6. If you don't have the luxury of automatic updates, you must manually upgrade WordPress. The most common reasons for automatic updates not working are incorrect permissions or the lack of an FTP server.

To manually upgrade, you'll need to visit `wordpress.org` and download the upgrade `.zip` or `.tar.gz` file. Open it up and extract the `wordpress` folder to your desktop.

Now in FileZilla, establish a connection to your host and make sure you're at the DocumentRoot for the domain/multisite network you're upgrading. The files on your host server will be displayed on the right-side of FileZilla. We'll use `/srv/www/multisite.longren.org/public_html/` as an example DocumentRoot.

On the left (local) side of FileZilla, navigate into the `wordpress` folder that we extracted earlier and select everything, including the `wp-admin`, `wp-content`, and `wp-includes` folders, along with all the files, including `wp-config-sample.php` and `wp-login.php`. Once everything is selected just drag it to your DocumentRoot folder on your webhost that's shown in the right-side of FileZilla, as seen in the following screenshot:

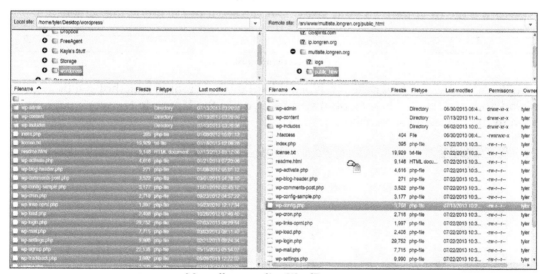

Manually upgrading WordPress core

After everything has transferred, you can go ahead and close FileZilla and delete that `wordpress` folder that's on your desktop.

I don't usually upgrade WordPress via FTP, I prefer to do it over SSH, mostly due to the fact that I have a relatively slow upload speed at home. If you'd prefer to upgrade via SSH, doing so is really easy. We'll use the same DocumentRoot example that we used above with FileZilla. I'm going to assume you know how to establish a connection to your server via SSH, and know that you need to press *Enter* after running the commands explained in the next paragraph. SSH is similar to Telnet but it's encrypted and is typically more responsive.

Make the connection to your server with your SSH client and download the latest version of WordPress with the `wget` command, by entering `wget http://wordpress.org/latest.tar.gz`. That will download a file named `latest.tar.gz` to your home directory. Decompress the `latest.tar.gz` file by entering `tar xfz latest.tar.gz`. After running that command, you should have a new folder in your home directory named `wordpress`. Now, run `cp -r wordpress/* /srv/www/multisite.longren.org/public_html/` to move the files in that `wordpress` folder to your DocumentRoot. And that's all there is to doing the same thing we did with FileZilla over SSH.

Now, navigate to your network dashboard; for me it would be `http://multisite.longren.org/wp-admin/`. Once you've logged in, you'll see a message at the top of your dashboard that says **Thank you for Updating! Please visit the Upgrade Network page to update all your sites**. You can see it in the following screenshot:

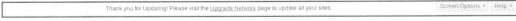

Upgrade Network notification

You'll notice that the **Upgrade Network** text in the previous screenshot is a link; go ahead and click on it. Clicking on it will take you to the **Upgrade Network** page, as seen in the following screenshot:

Upgrade Network page

There's a button on that page that also reads **Upgrade Network**. Go ahead and click on the **Upgrade Network** button to start the database upgrade process. If everything has gone well, you should end up at a page that says **All done!**, as you see in the following screenshot:

All done! with database upgrade

Updating plugins and themes

This is one of the things I love most about WordPress multisite. It makes updating everything all at once really, really easy.

Plugins and themes can be updated as usual through the **Updates** page in the network dashboard as seen in the following screenshot. If you can't upgrade the WordPress core automatically, you probably can't update themes or plugins automatically, either. If that's the case, you can update plugins and themes manually just as you would on a regular WordPress installation; just copy the updated plugin or theme folder to `wp-content/themes` for themes, or `wp-content/plugins` for plugins. You can do this via FTP using FileZilla, or you can do it via SSH by downloading the updates, decompressing them, and copying the updated folders to their various destinations, as mentioned in the previous section.

Available Updates

Resources

There are some really great resources out there for WordPress; `wordpress.org` alone hosts a mountain of information, from the WordPress Codex to the community forums.

The Codex hosts basically every piece of documentation there is for WordPress. It covers literally everything that WordPress has to offer.

The community forums have a subforum specifically aimed at multisite installations. You can find it at `http://wordpress.org/support/forum/multisite/`.

There are also many third-party resources, such as **WPMU** (WordPress MU) , at `http://wpmu.org/`. It became incredibly popular within the WordPress community before WordPress 3.0 was available, so the "MU" in WPMU is a throwback to the pre 3.0 WordPress feature called Multi-User that essentially morphed into what multisite is today. They have a great explanation at `http://wpmu.org/about/`.

I've compiled a list of resources in the following table:

URL	Name/description
`http://codex.wordpress.org/Main_Page`	This is the WordPress Codex. It contains all the documentation.
`http://wordpress.org/support/forum/multisite/`	It contains the WordPress multisite forum.
`http://wordpress.org/support//`	It contains the main WordPress support forums.
`http://wpmu.org/`	This is WPMU, which is a private, third-party multisite resource.
`http://mashable.com/2012/07/26/beginner-guide-wordpress-multisite/`	It contains a beginner's guide from Mashable.
`http://wiki.dreamhost.com/WordPress_Multisite`	It contains Wordpress multisite information. Just general, good information to have.
`http://halfelf.org/2012/moving-wordpress-multisite/`	It contains an article on Moving WordPress Multisite, from *Mika Epstein*, a WordPress contributor.
`http://codex.wordpress.org/Before_You_Create_A_Network`	It contains the WordPress Codex article listing some multisite requirements.

URL	Name/description
`http://wpcandy.com/presents/an-introduction-to-wordpress-multisite/`	It is another nice high level overview helping people understand multisite.
`http://wordpress.stackexchange.com/`	It is a great resource for finding answers to common questions, or posting your own questions if necessary.
`http://wp.smashingmagazine.com/`	It contains the Smashing Magazine site dedicated to WordPress.
`http://speckyboy.com/category/wordpress/`	It contains the WordPress articles from the Specyboy Design Magazine.
`http://planet.wordpress.org/`	It contains posts from various WordPress contributors.

That is really a pretty small list of resources. Google is always a pretty valuable resource, searching for WordPress multisite yields about 1.1 million results, but this may vary from person to person due to user-tailored search results.

Summary

Troubleshooting WordPress can be a pain sometimes, just as with troubleshooting anything. We went through a few of the most common issues and how to troubleshoot them. There's also a short but excellent list of resources to help you out. Now that you know what to use for backups, how to update WordPress core, and how to update themes and plugins, your site should be good to go. Just make sure to test at least one backup to make sure everything is working.

Index

Thank you for buying
WordPress Multisite Administration

About Packt Publishing

Packt, pronounced 'packed', published its first book "*Mastering phpMyAdmin for Effective MySQL Management*" in April 2004 and subsequently continued to specialize in publishing highly focused books on specific technologies and solutions.

Our books and publications share the experiences of your fellow IT professionals in adapting and customizing today's systems, applications, and frameworks. Our solution based books give you the knowledge and power to customize the software and technologies you're using to get the job done. Packt books are more specific and less general than the IT books you have seen in the past. Our unique business model allows us to bring you more focused information, giving you more of what you need to know, and less of what you don't.

Packt is a modern, yet unique publishing company, which focuses on producing quality, cutting-edge books for communities of developers, administrators, and newbies alike. For more information, please visit our website: www.packtpub.com.

About Packt Open Source

In 2010, Packt launched two new brands, Packt Open Source and Packt Enterprise, in order to continue its focus on specialization. This book is part of the Packt Open Source brand, home to books published on software built around Open Source licences, and offering information to anybody from advanced developers to budding web designers. The Open Source brand also runs Packt's Open Source Royalty Scheme, by which Packt gives a royalty to each Open Source project about whose software a book is sold.

Writing for Packt

We welcome all inquiries from people who are interested in authoring. Book proposals should be sent to author@packtpub.com. If your book idea is still at an early stage and you would like to discuss it first before writing a formal book proposal, contact us; one of our commissioning editors will get in touch with you.

We're not just looking for published authors; if you have strong technical skills but no writing experience, our experienced editors can help you develop a writing career, or simply get some additional reward for your expertise.

WordPress Theme Development - Beginner's Guide

ISBN: 978-1-84951-422-4   Paperback: 252 pages

Learn how to deign and build great
WordPress themes

1. Learn how to design WordPress themes and
   build them from scratch

2. Learn how to create a WordPress theme design
   using HTML5 and CSS3

3. With clear and easy to follow worked examples
   to help you build your first WordPress theme if
   you've never done it before

WordPress for Education

ISBN: 978-1-84951-820-8   Paperback: 144 pages

Create interactive and engaging e-learning websites
with WordPress

1. Develop effective e-learning websites that will
   engage your students

2. Extend the potential of a classroom website
   with WordPress plugins

3. Create an interactive social network and course
   management system to enhance student and
   instructor communication

Please check **www.PacktPub.com** for information on our titles

Social Media for WordPress: Beginner's Guide

ISBN: 978-1-84719-980-5 Paperback: 166 pages

A quicker way to build communities, engage members, and promote your site

1. Integrate automated key marketing techniques

2. Examine analytical data to measure social engagement

3. Understand the core principles of establishing meaningful social connections

WordPress 3 Complete

ISBN: 978-1-84951-410-1 Paperback: 344 pages

Create your own complete website or blog from scratch with WordPress

1. Learn everything you need for creating your own feature-rich website or blog from scratch

2. Clear and practical explanations of all aspects of WordPress

3. In-depth coverage of installation, themes, plugins, and syndication

4. Explore WordPress as a fully functional content management system

Please check **www.PacktPub.com** for information on our titles

www.ingramcontent.com/pod-product-compliance
Lightning Source LLC
Chambersburg PA
CBHW060200060326
40690CB00018B/4193